God Has A Plan For Your Life
A Bible Verses Coloring Book
An Adult Coloring Book Of Bible Verses
On Success And God's Amazing Plan For Your Life!

By
Ethlyn MacDonald

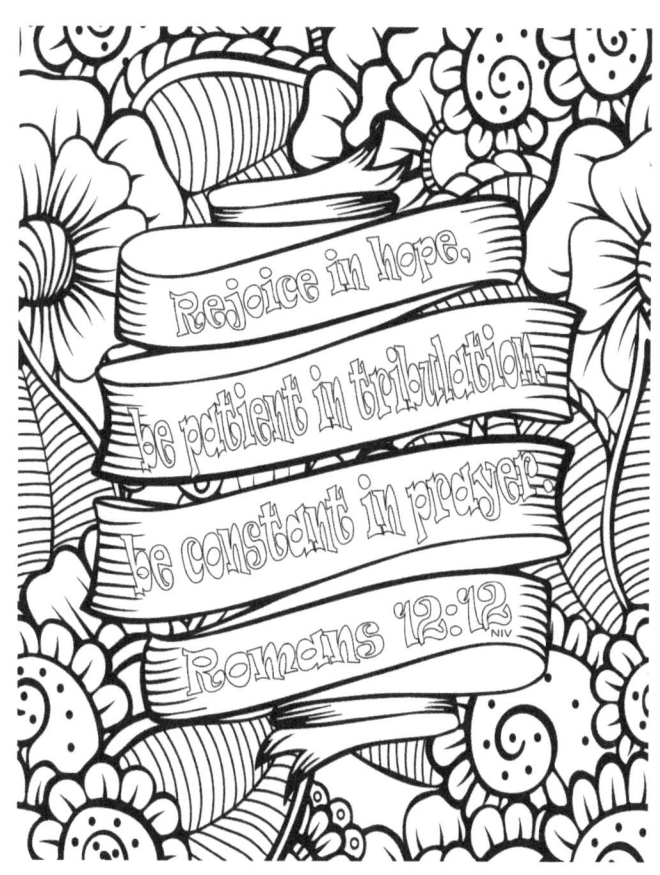

ISBN-10:1548897167
ISBN-13:978-1548897161

ABOUT THE DESIGN OF MY COLORING BOOKS

COMPLEXITY: When I was facing cancer and going through chemotherapy, I renewed my interest in coloring. I was frustrated by trying to find coloring books that had different levels of complexity and styles.   I design my books for a variety of coloring enthusiasts.

-A third of the designs are complex,
-A third of the designs are medium complexity.
-A third of the designs are simpler for when you want to color but you have less time and don't want an overwhelming project to complete.

It is my hope that by providing a multitude of complexity and design styles, coloring can be fun, therapeutic, and frustration free for all!

BLOTTING PAGES: At the end of the book you will find blotting pages. When self-publishing, Independent authors are not given a choice of paper thickness nor given the option of perforating the pages for easy Removal. Possibly in the future, the printers will let us have those Features because we know how important they are.

The blotting pages should help you to be able to use markers if you so
Compendium Of Included Designs
desire without ruining the pages underneath. Simply remove one and slip it underneath the design.

You can also use the pages to test and keep track of your color choices. No more losing your test scrap paper before you complete your design and having to guess which color you used! I hate that! If you are the artistic type, feel free to use the space for designs of your own!

Compendium Of Included Designs

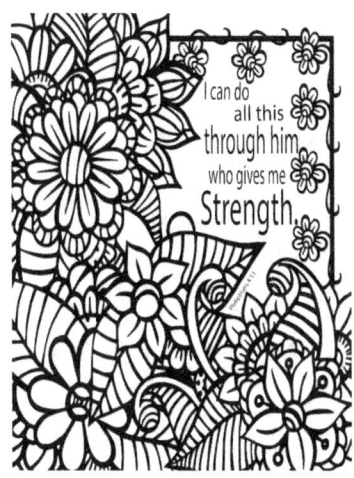

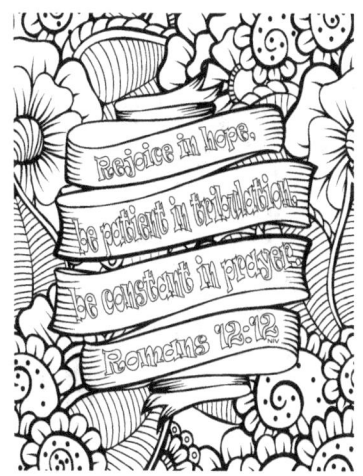

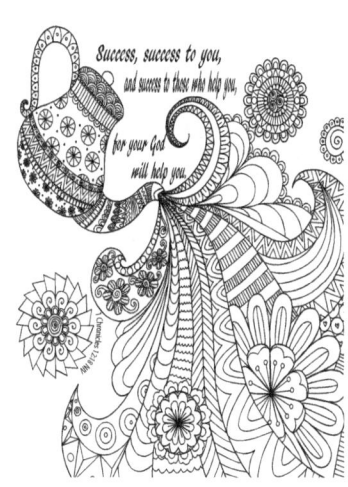

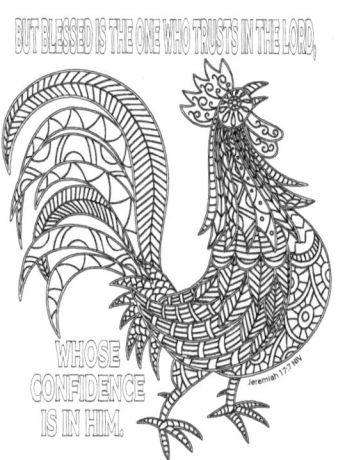

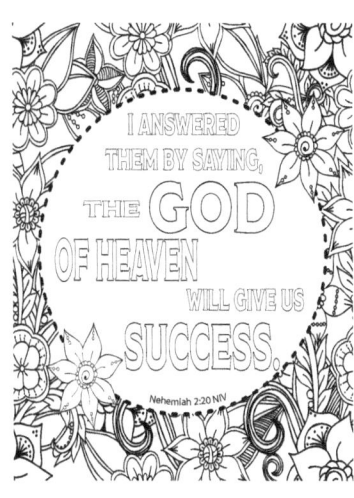

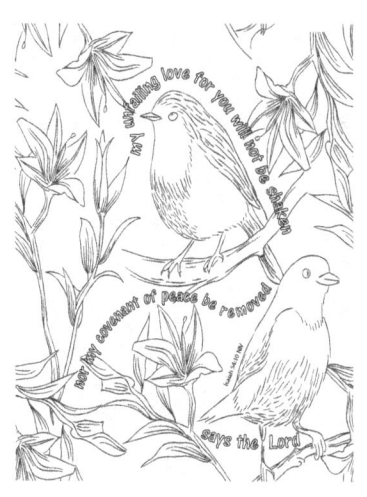

Compendium Of Included Designs

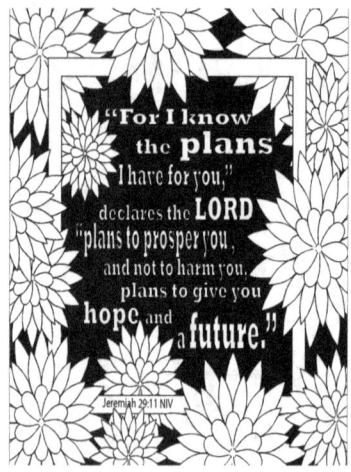

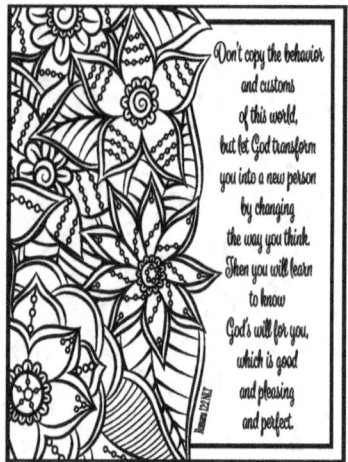

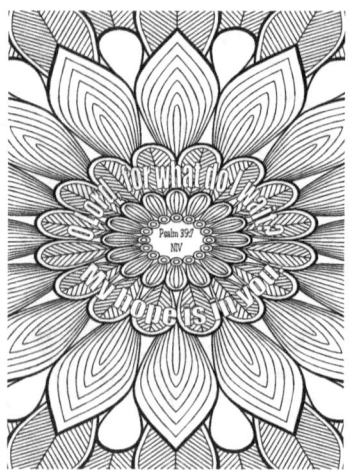

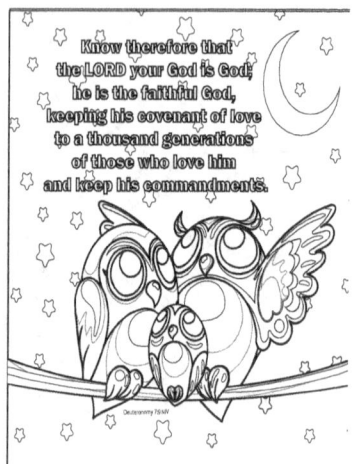

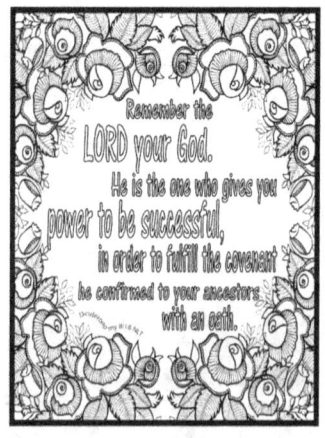

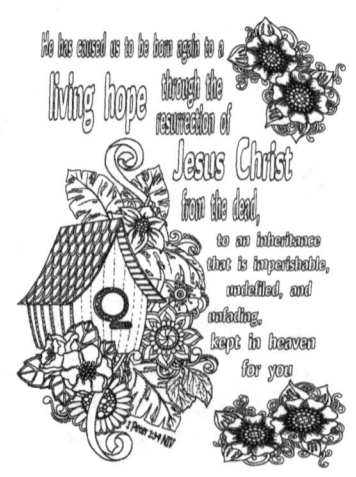

Compendium Of Included Designs

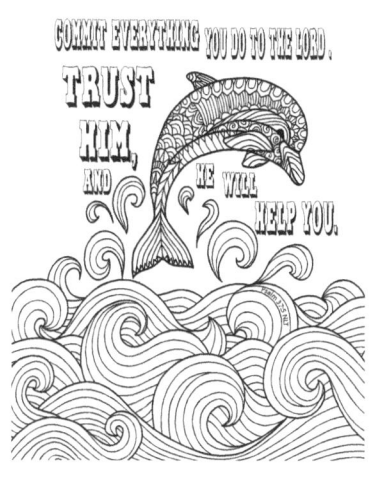

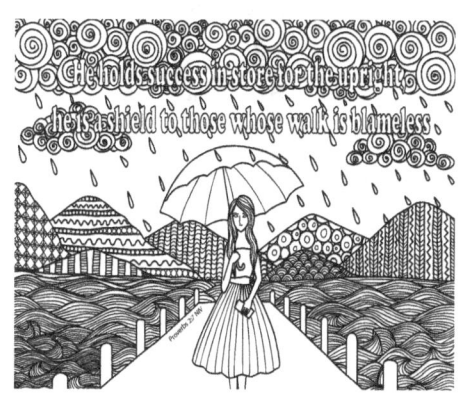

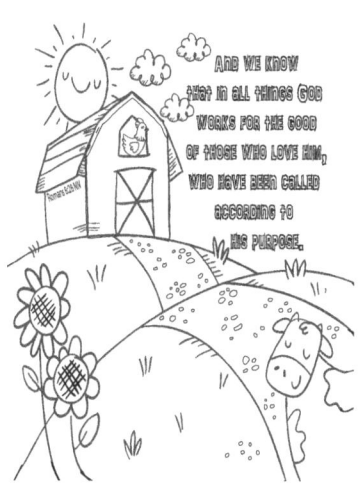

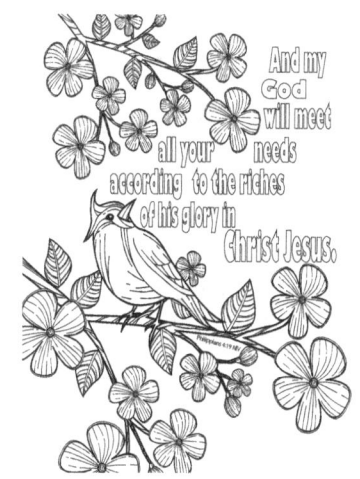

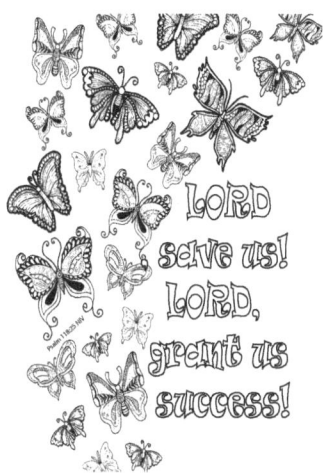

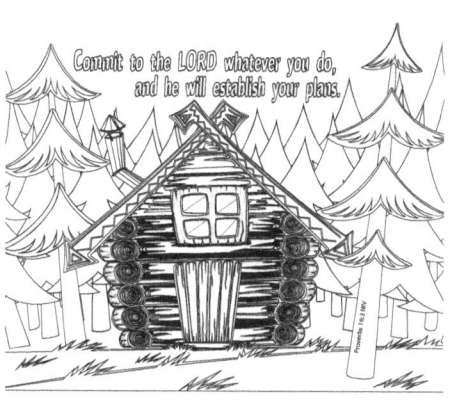

Compendium Of Included Designs

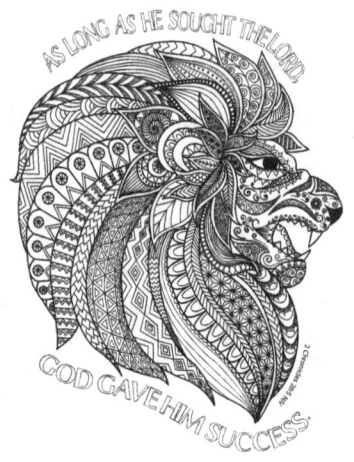

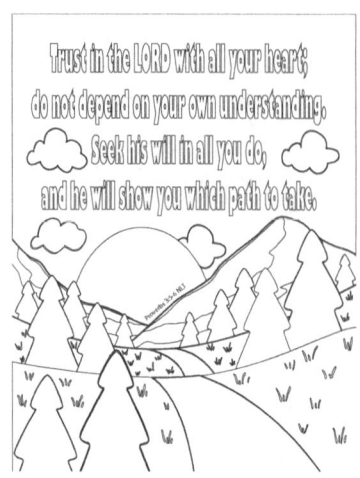

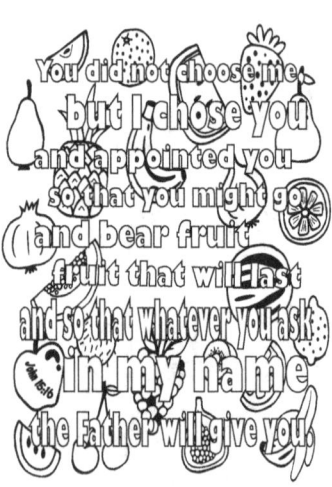

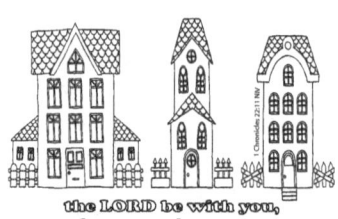

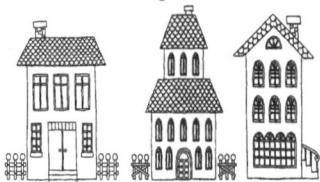

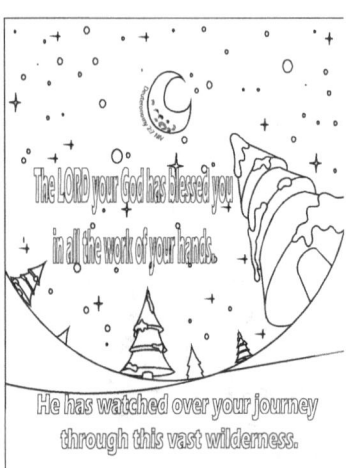

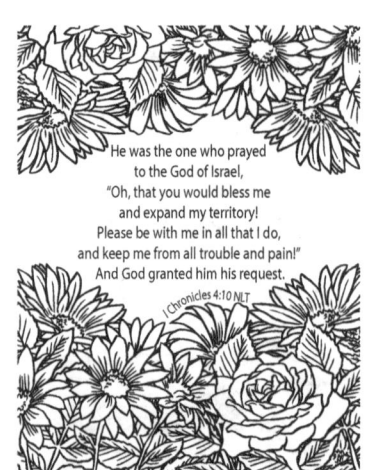

Compendium Of Included Designs

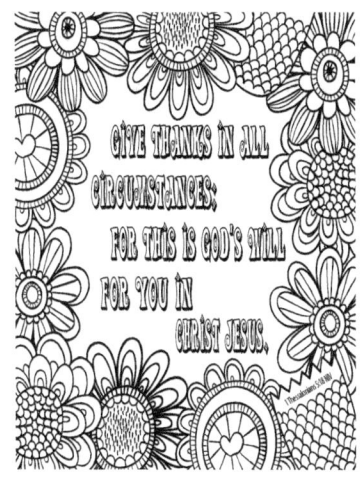

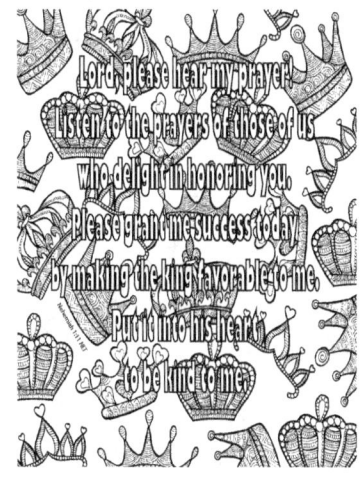

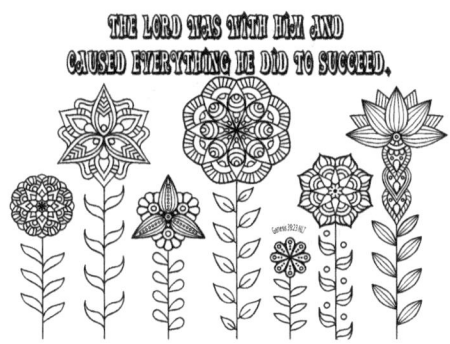

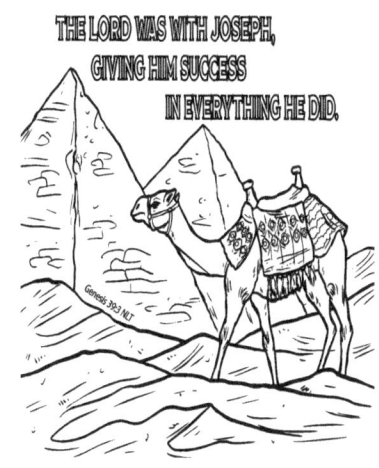

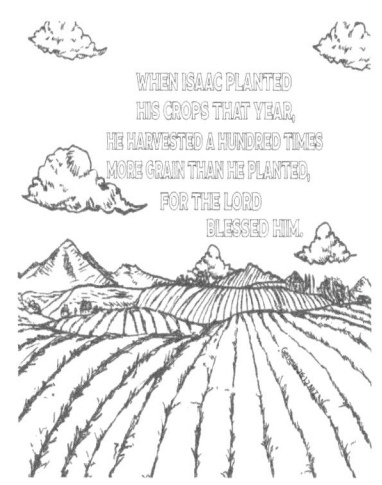

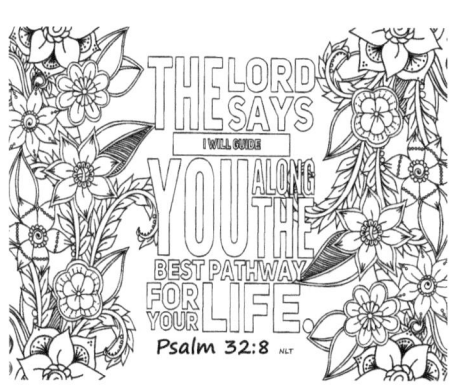

Compendium Of Included Designs

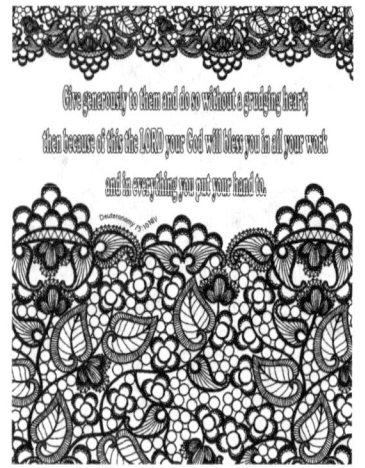

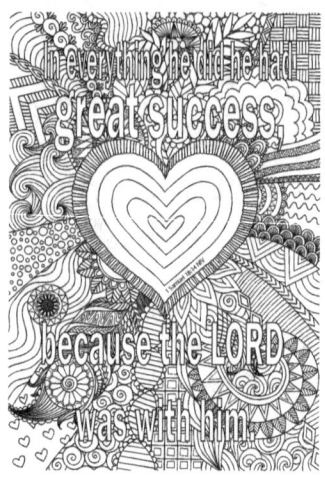

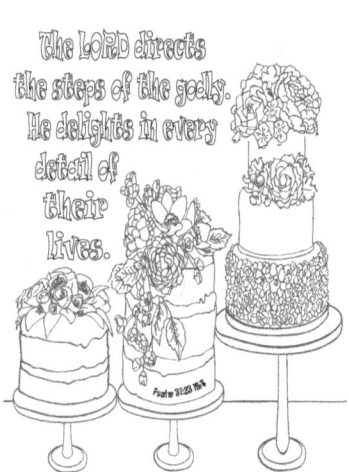

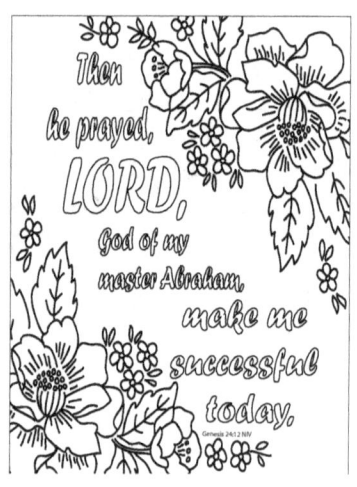

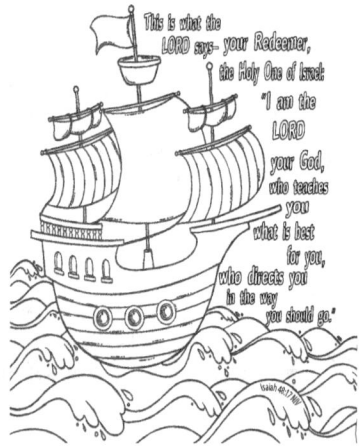

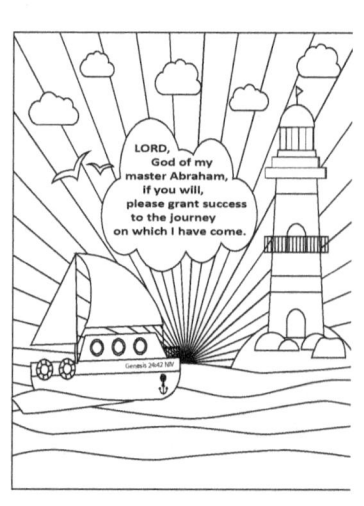

Compendium Of Included Designs

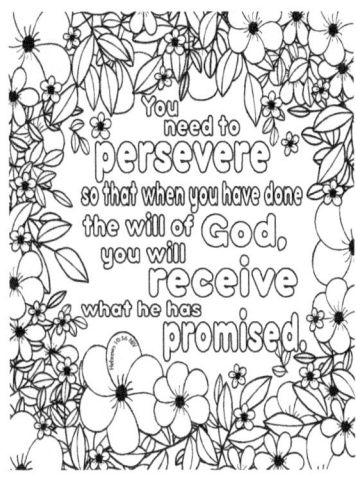

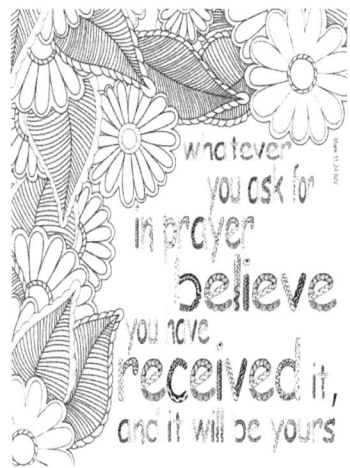

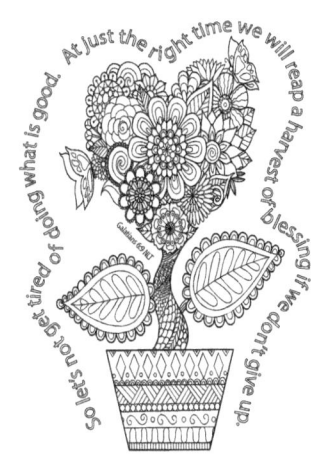

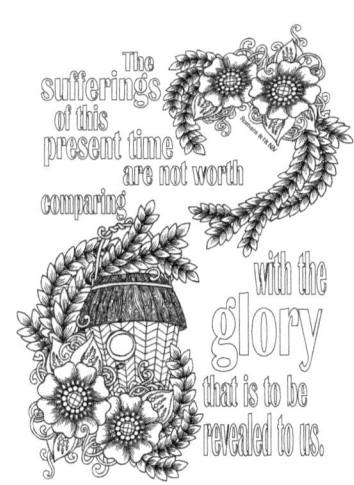

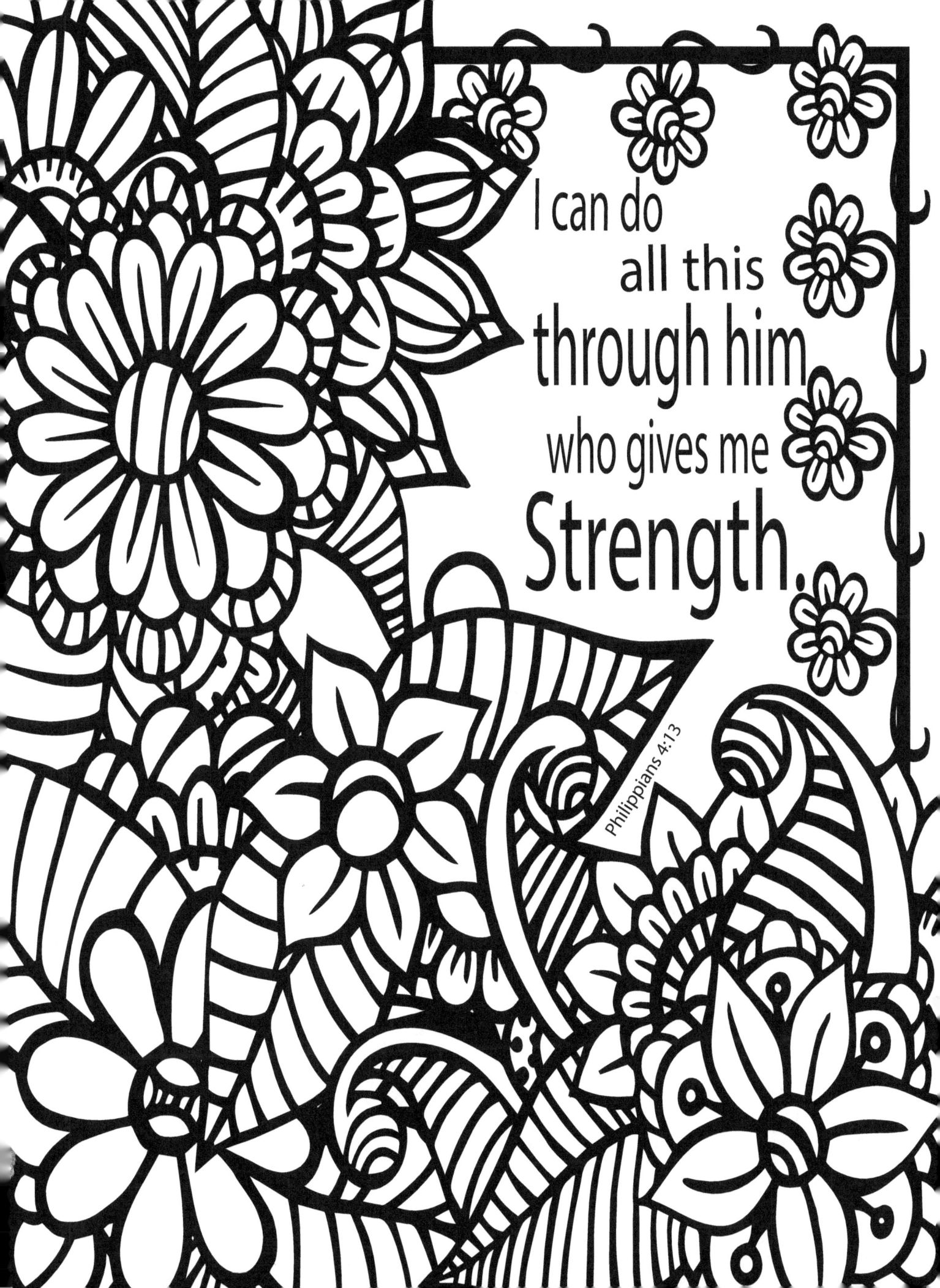

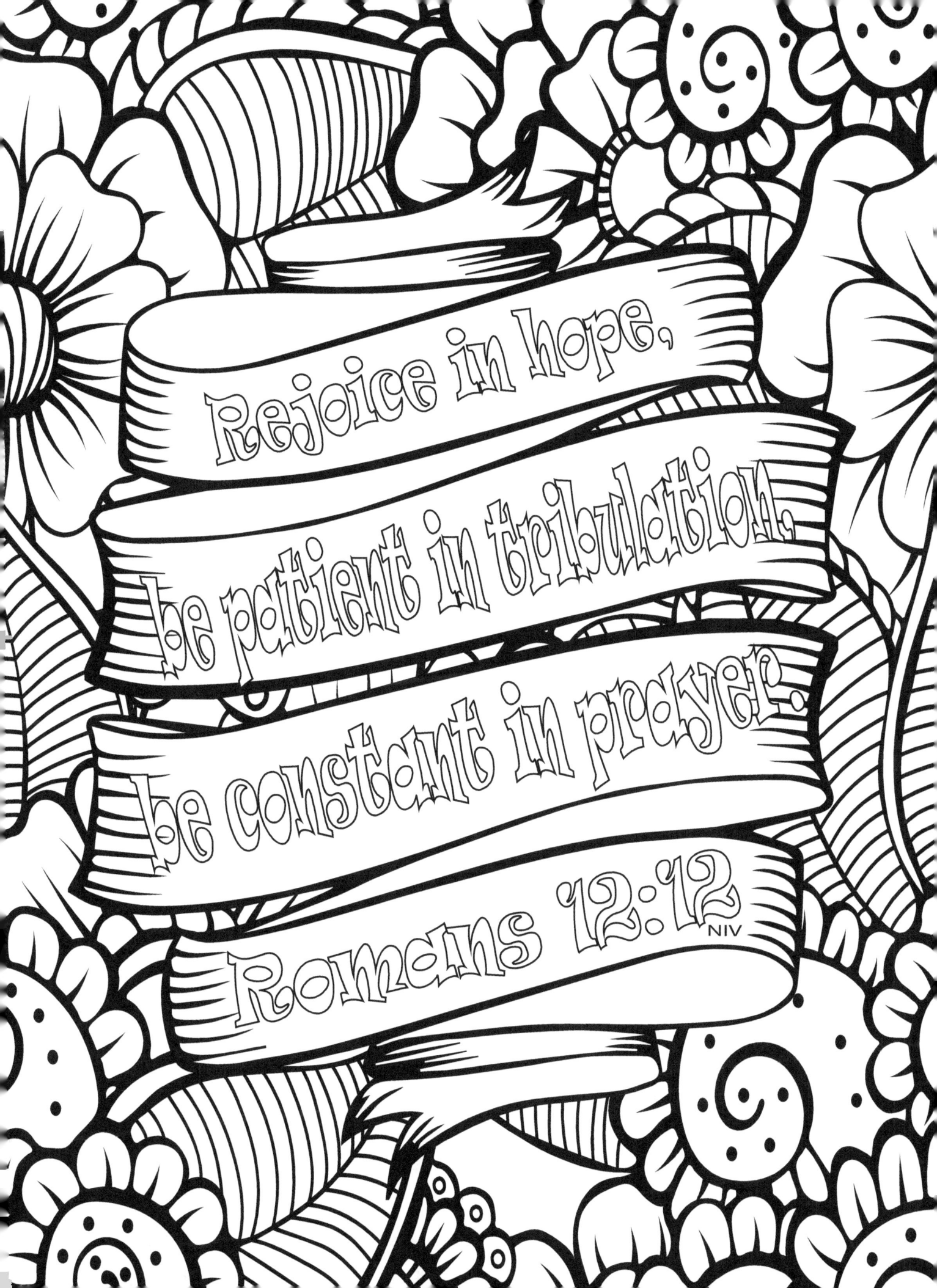

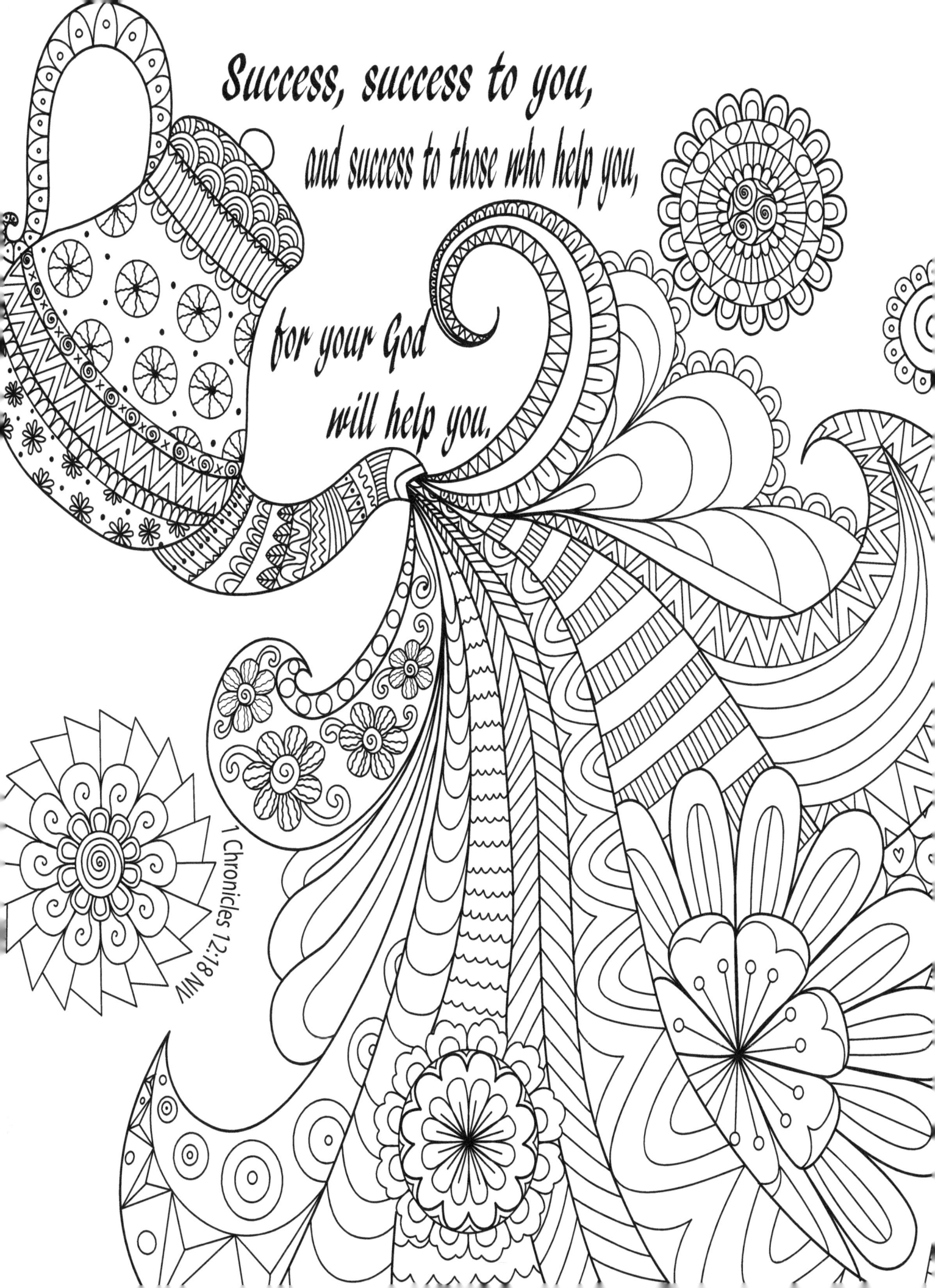

Success, success to you,
and success to those who help you,

for your God
will help you,

1 Chronicles 12:18 NIV

BUT BLESSED IS THE ONE WHO TRUSTS IN THE LORD,

WHOSE CONFIDENCE IS IN HIM.

Jeremiah 17:7 NIV

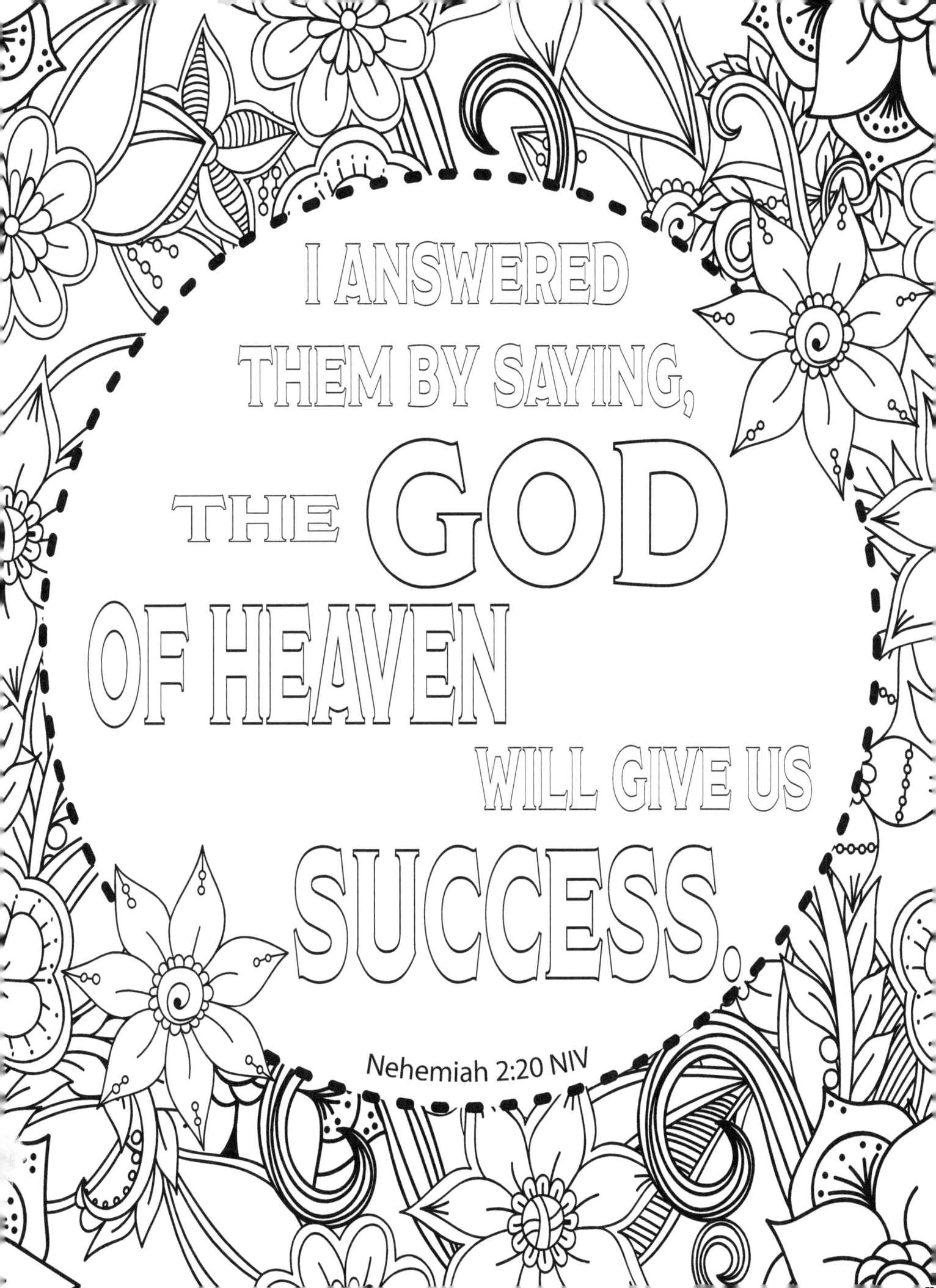

I ANSWERED THEM BY SAYING, THE GOD OF HEAVEN WILL GIVE US SUCCESS.

Nehemiah 2:20 NIV

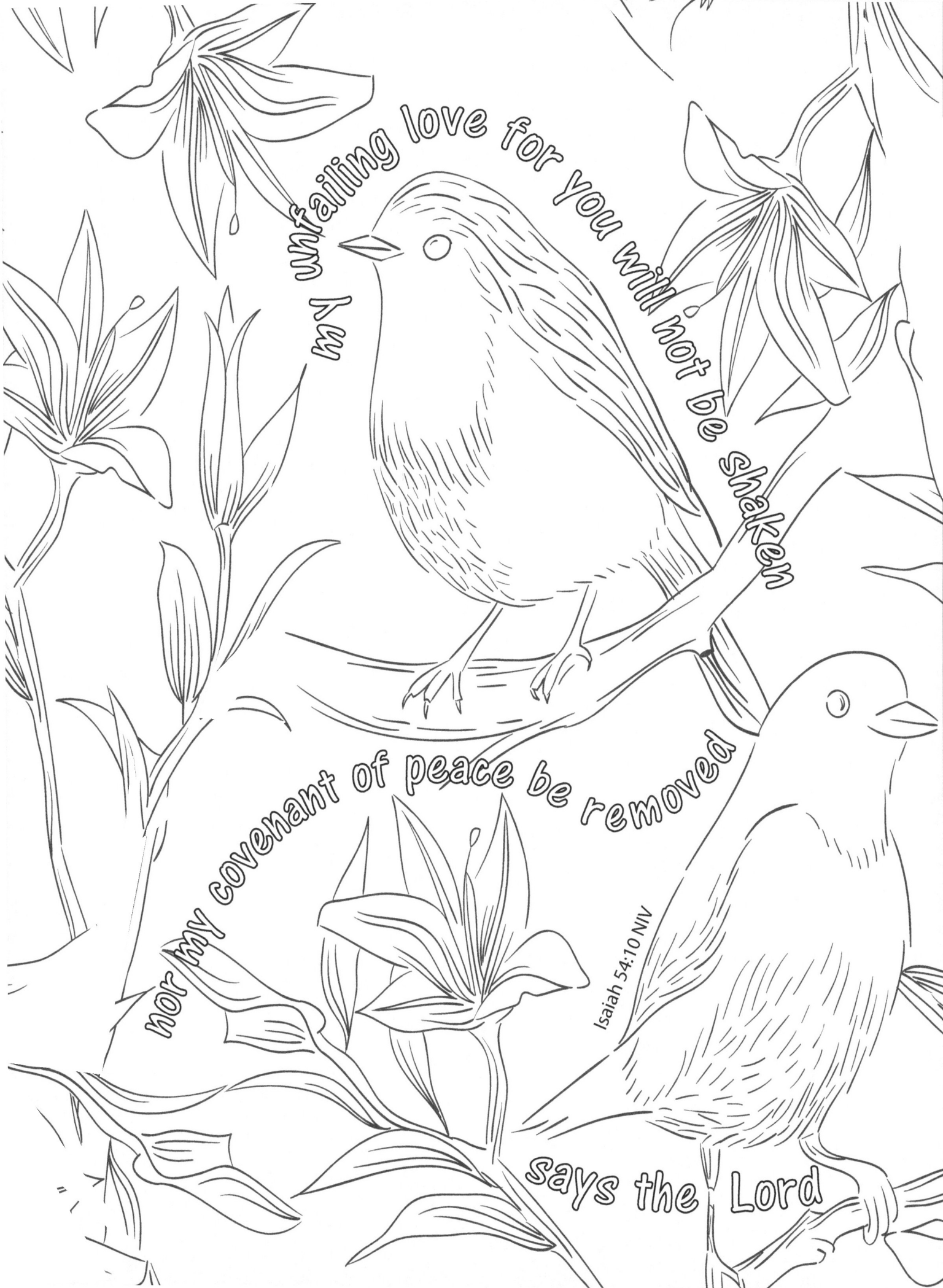

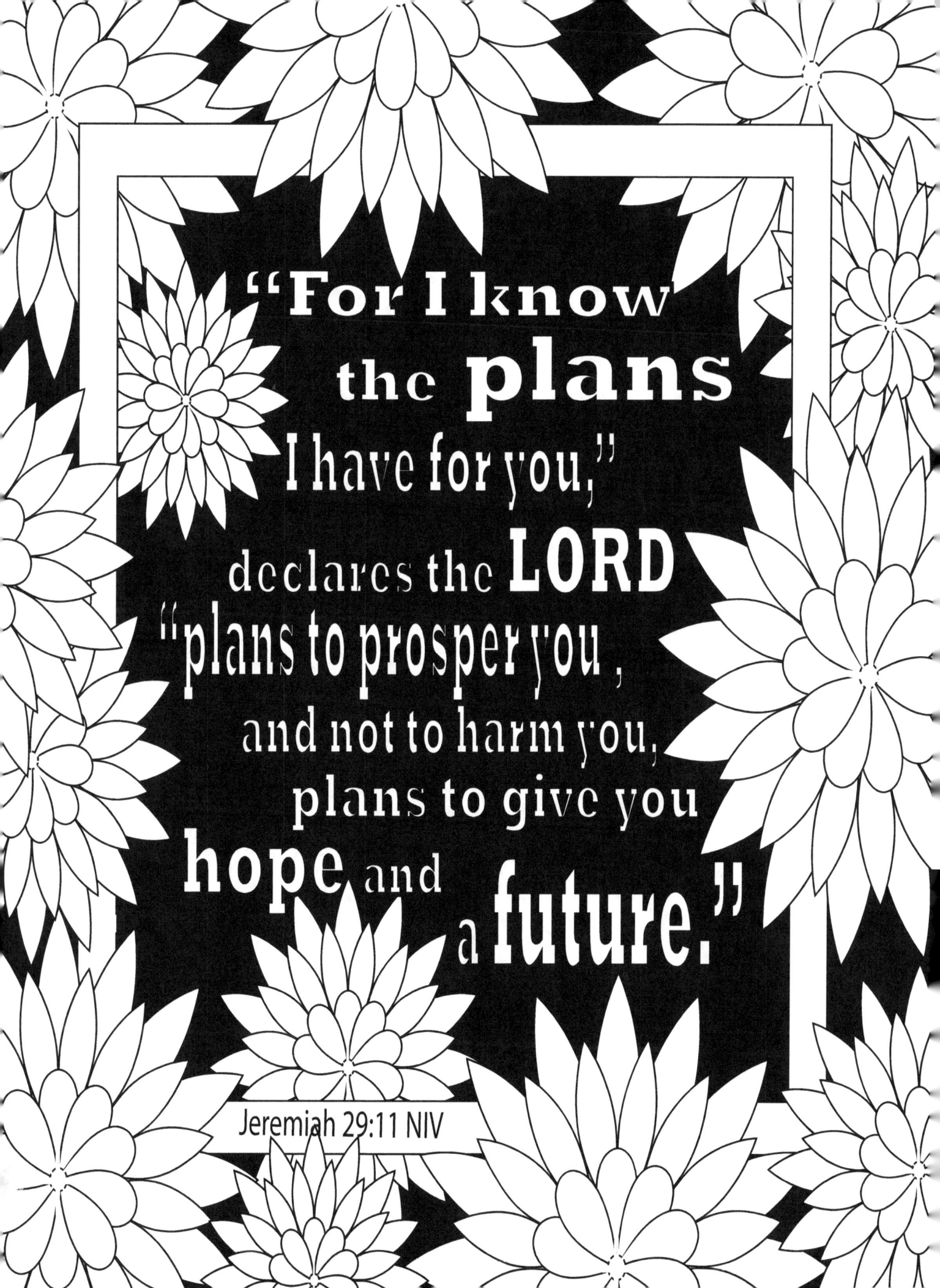

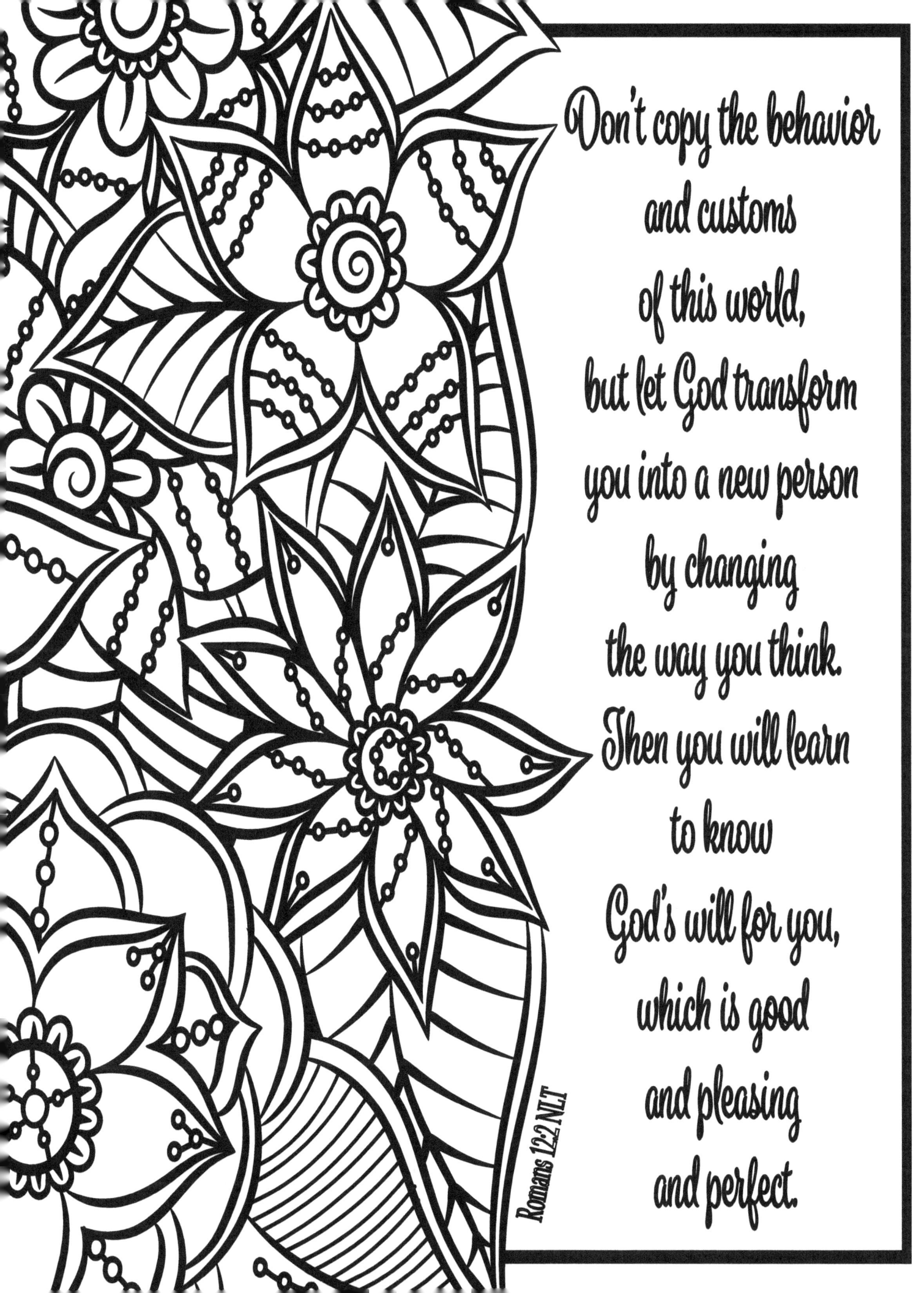

Don't copy the behavior and customs of this world, but let God transform you into a new person by changing the way you think. Then you will learn to know God's will for you, which is good and pleasing and perfect.

Romans 12:2 NLT

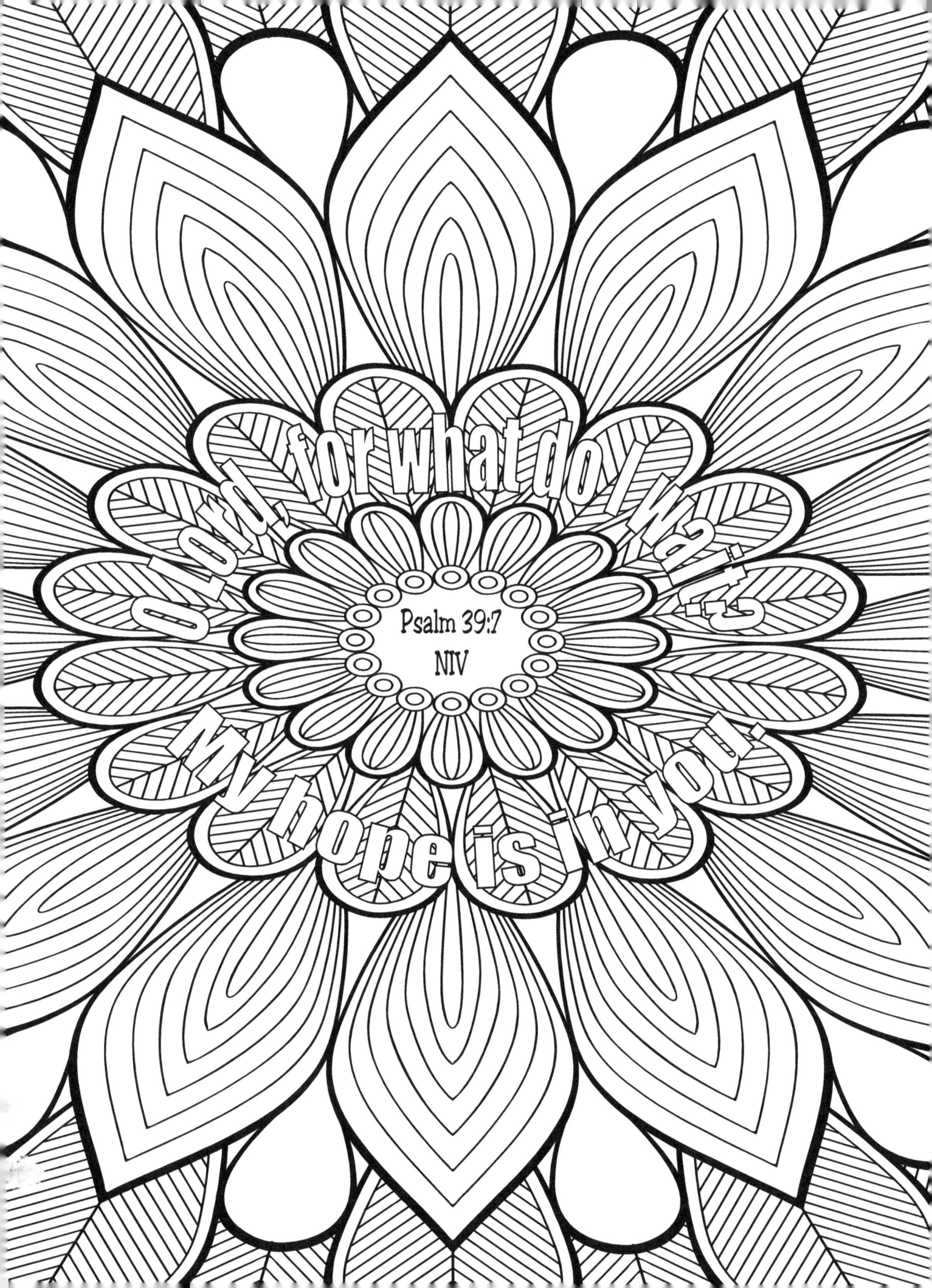

O Lord, for what do I wait? My hope is in you.

Psalm 39:7
NIV

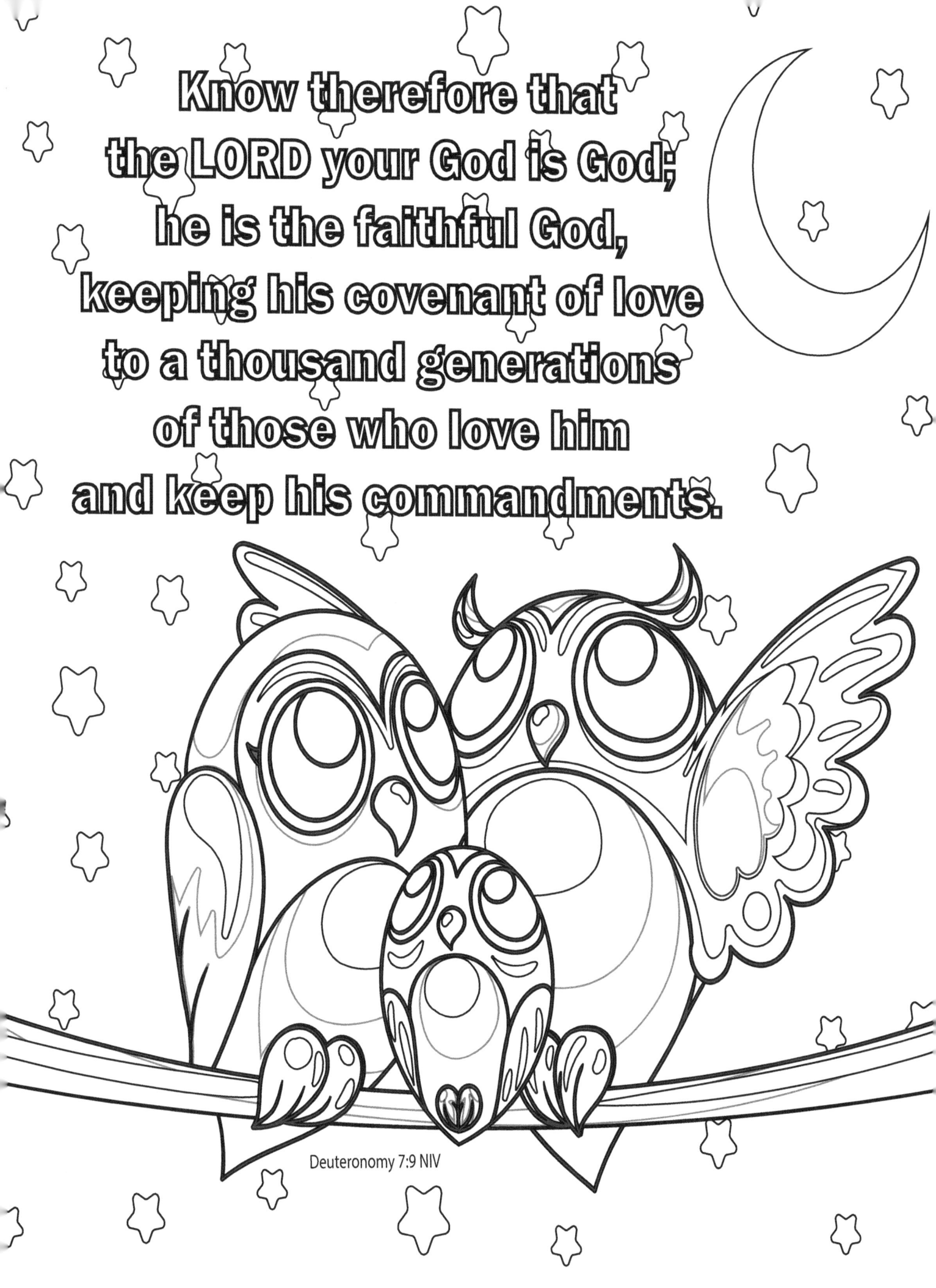

Know therefore that the LORD your God is God; he is the faithful God, keeping his covenant of love to a thousand generations of those who love him and keep his commandments.

Deuteronomy 7:9 NIV

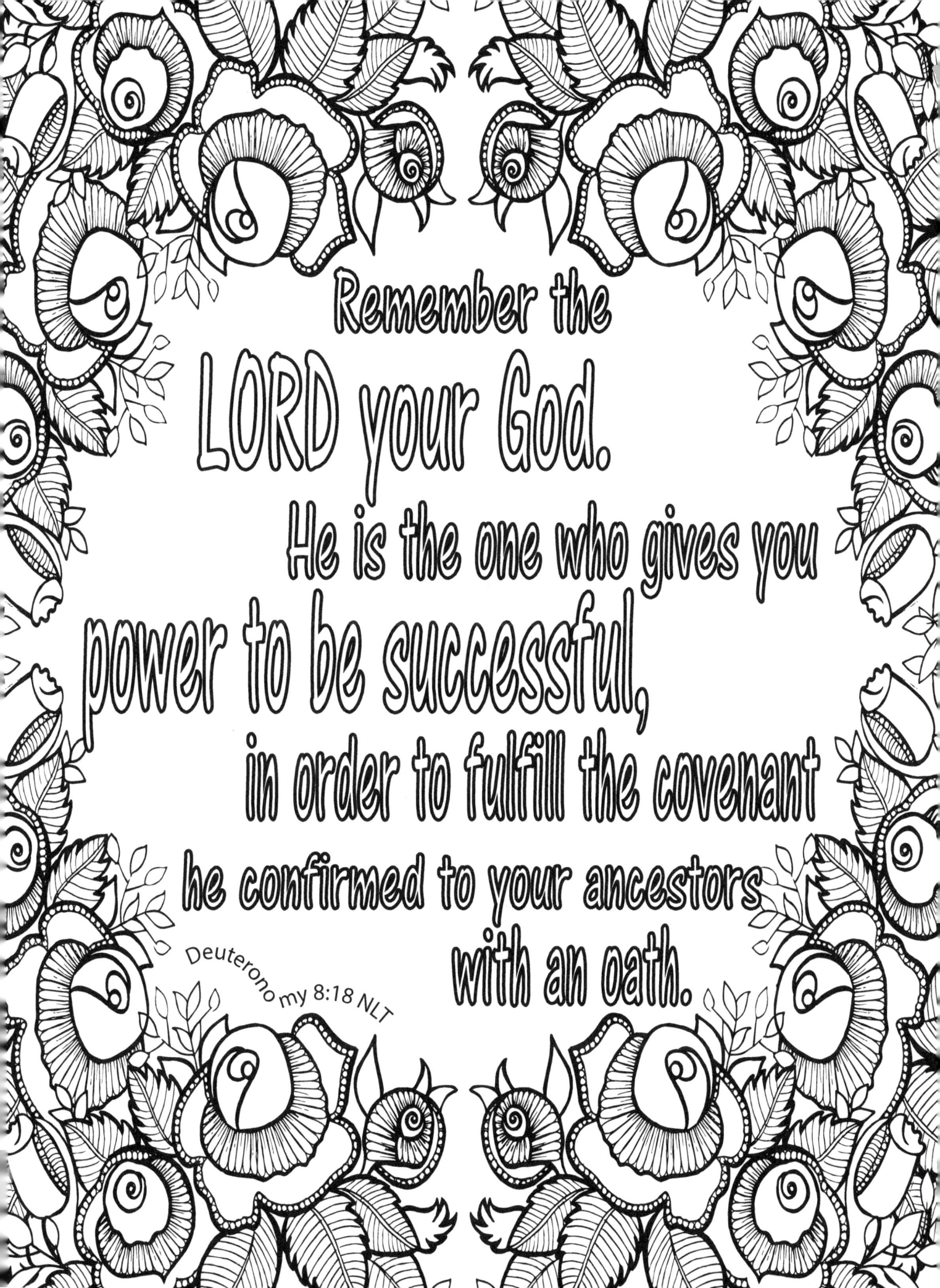

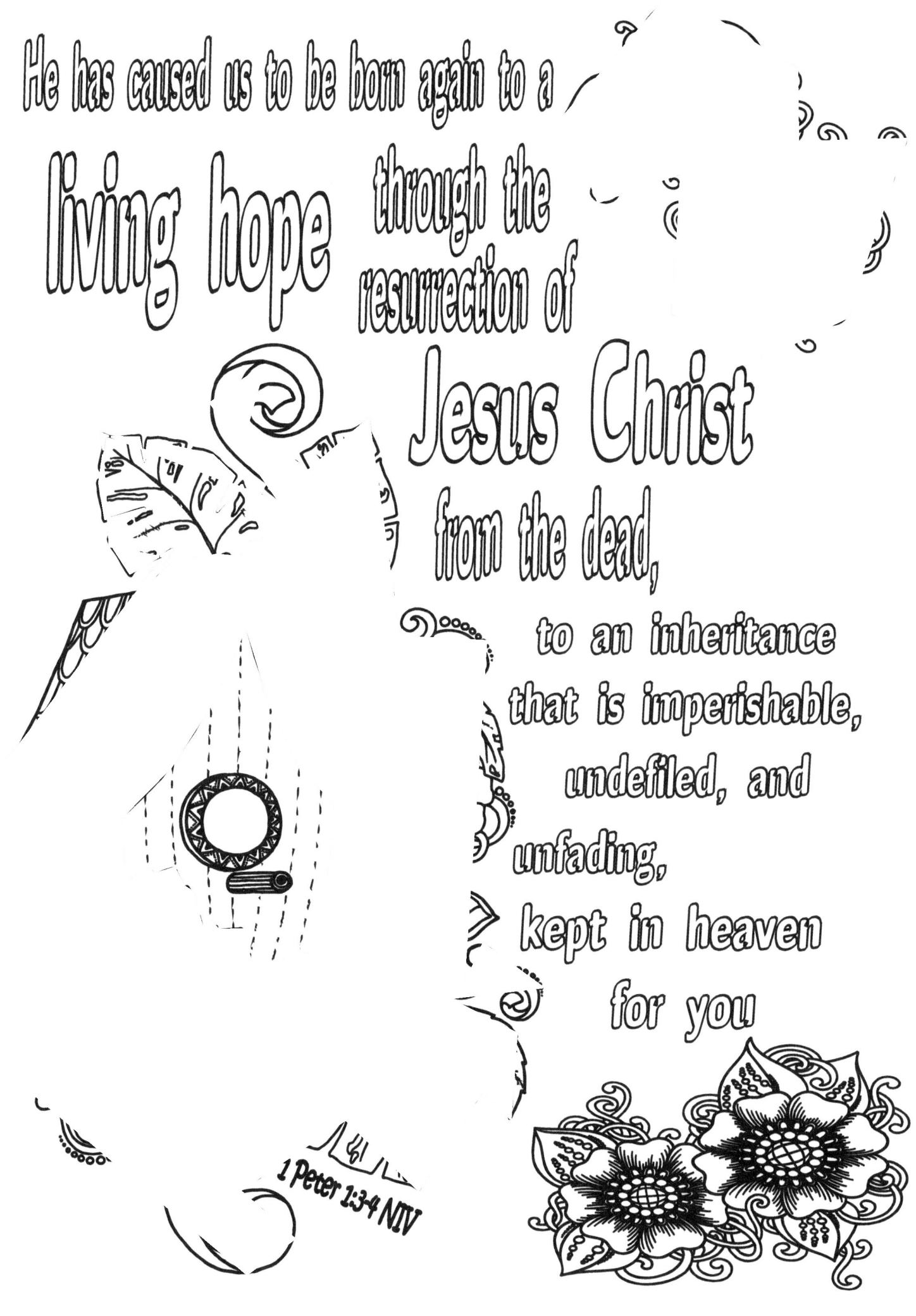

He has caused us to be born again to a **living hope** through the resurrection of **Jesus Christ** from the dead, to an inheritance that is imperishable, undefiled, and unfading, kept in heaven for you

1 Peter 1:3-4 NIV

COMMIT EVERYTHING YOU DO TO THE LORD.
TRUST HIM, AND HE WILL HELP YOU.

Psalm 37:5 NLT

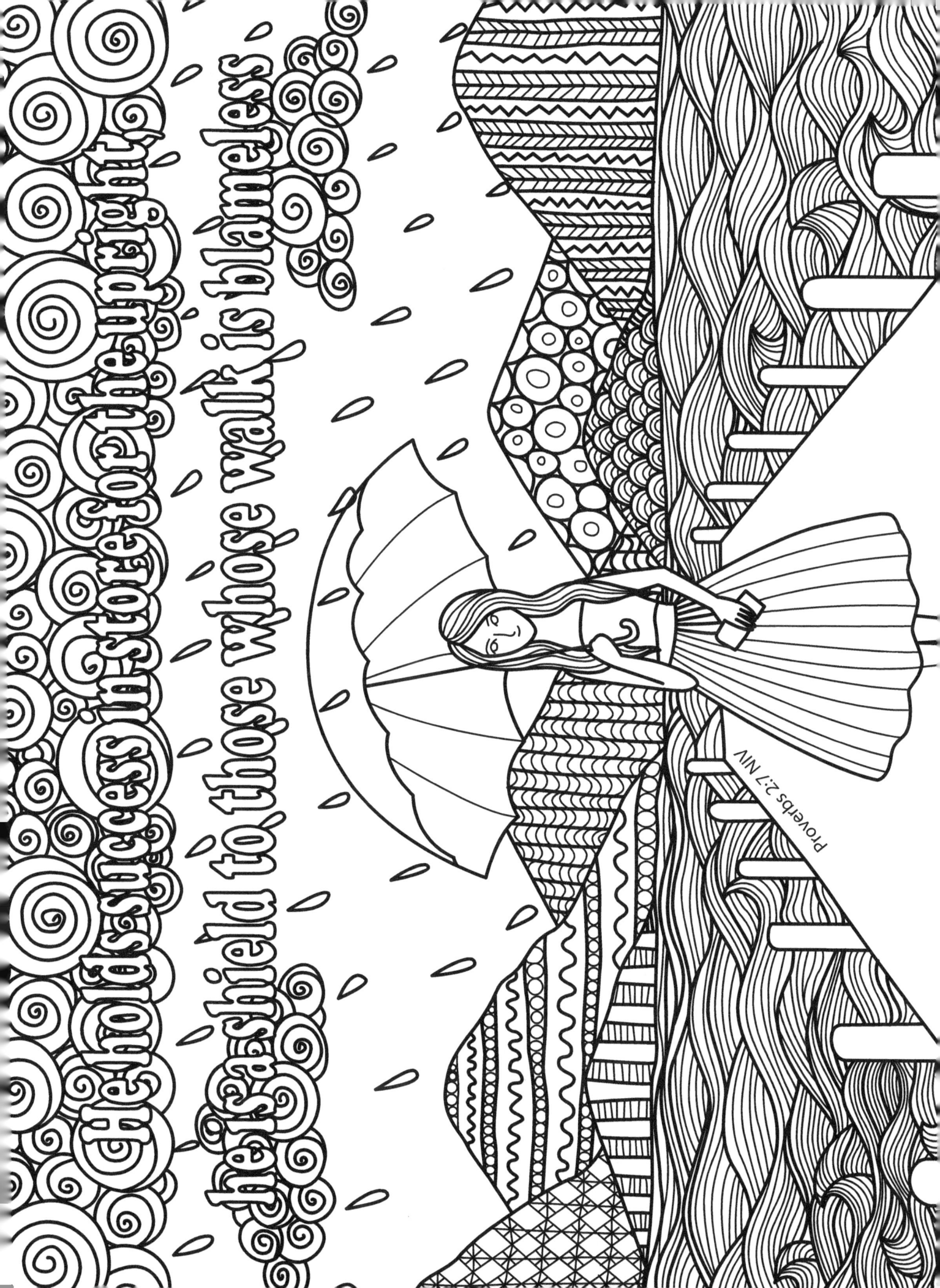

He holds success in store for the upright, he is a shield to those whose walk is blameless

Proverbs 2:7 NIV

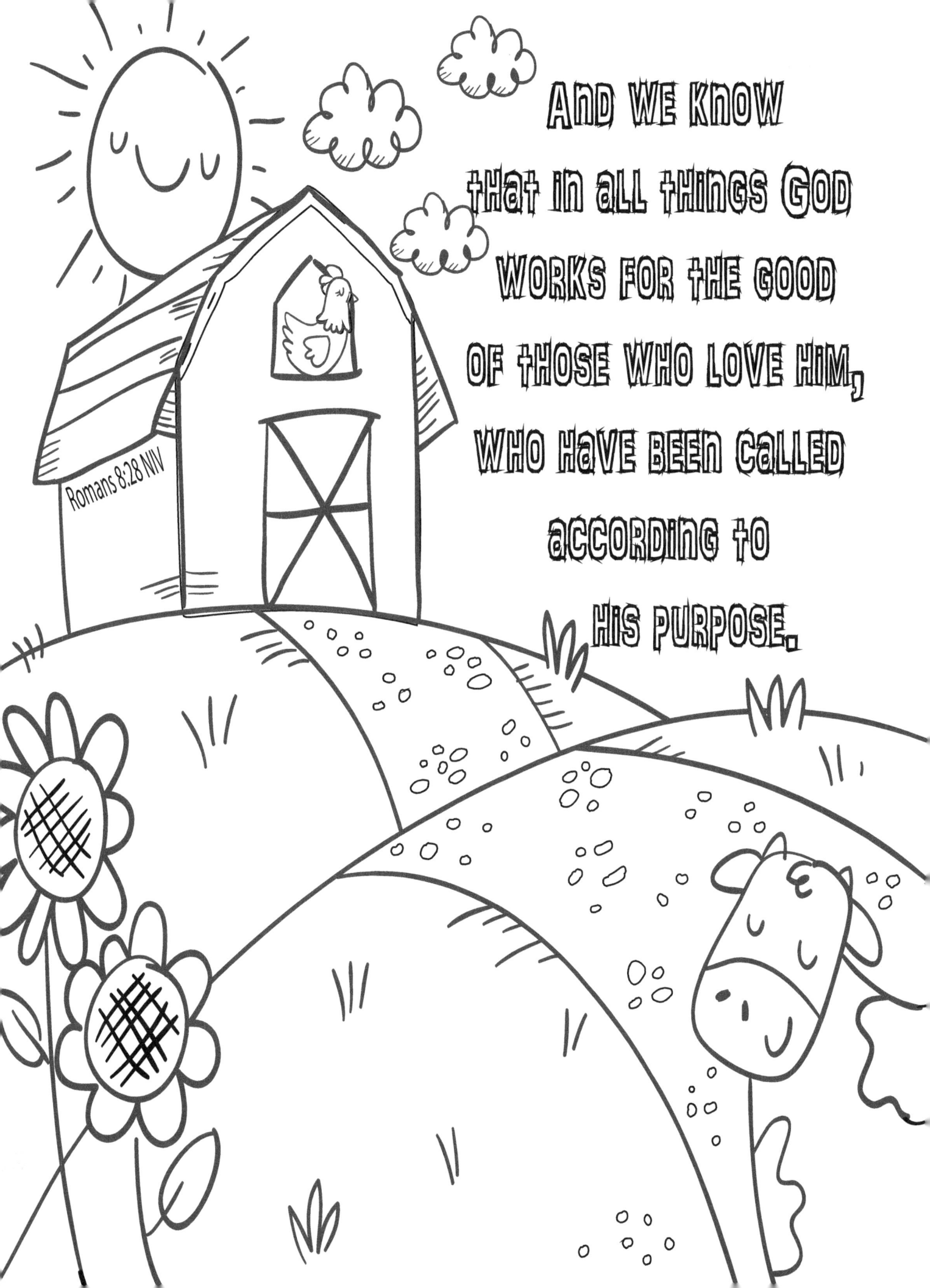

And we know that in all things God works for the good of those who love him, who have been called according to his purpose.

Romans 8:28 NIV

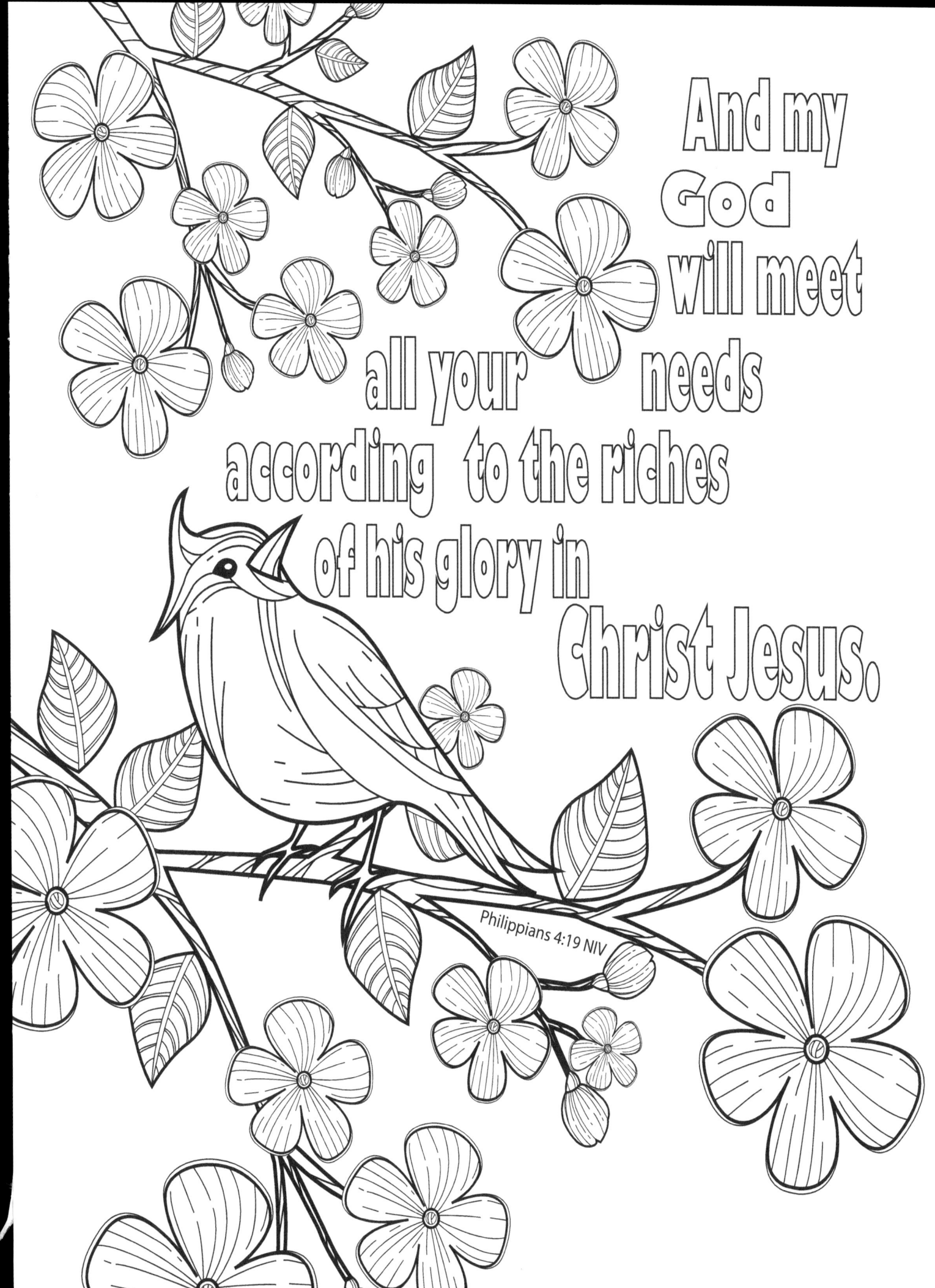

And my God will meet all your needs according to the riches of his glory in Christ Jesus.

Philippians 4:19 NIV

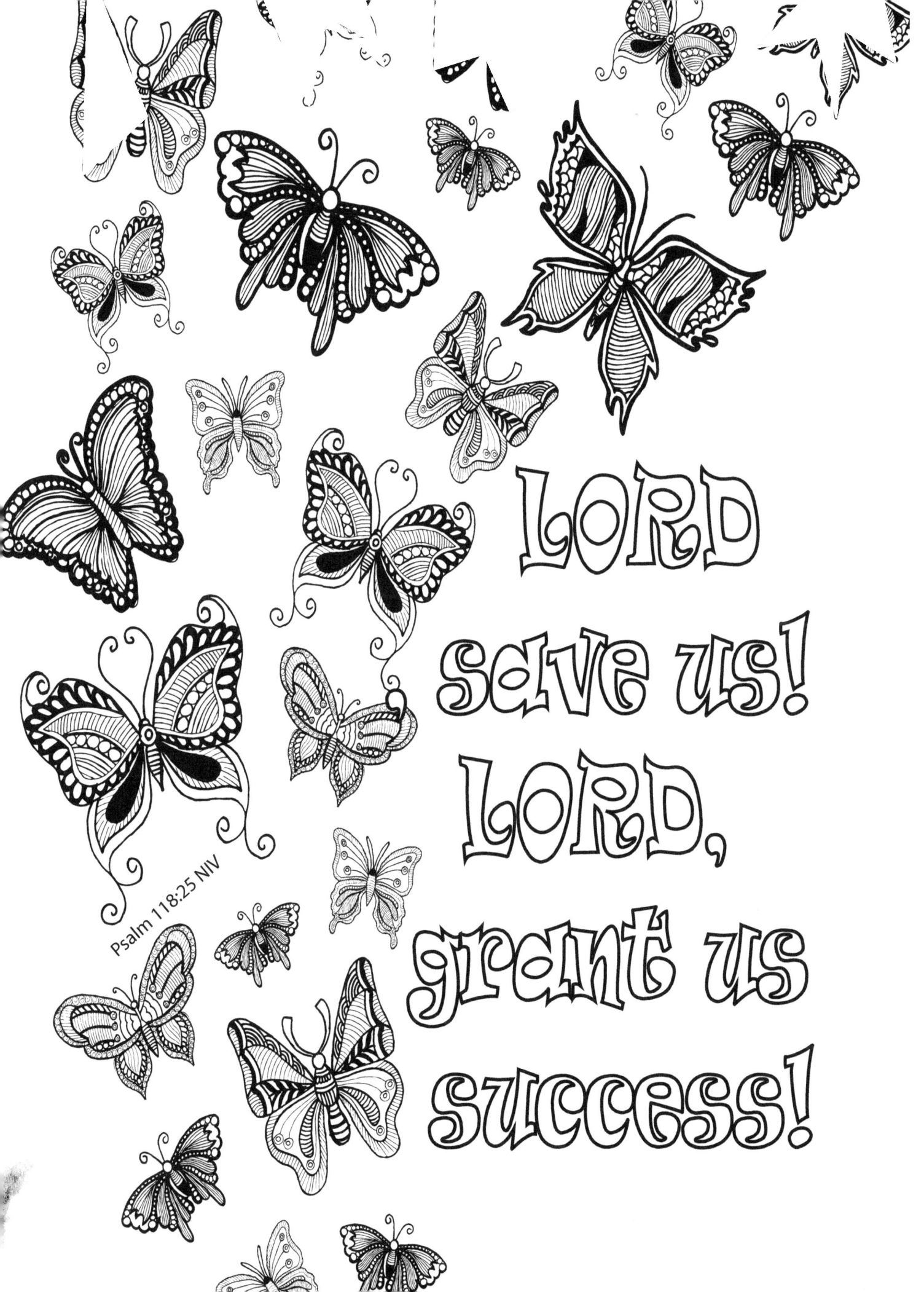

Psalm 118:25 NIV

LORD save us! LORD, grant us success!

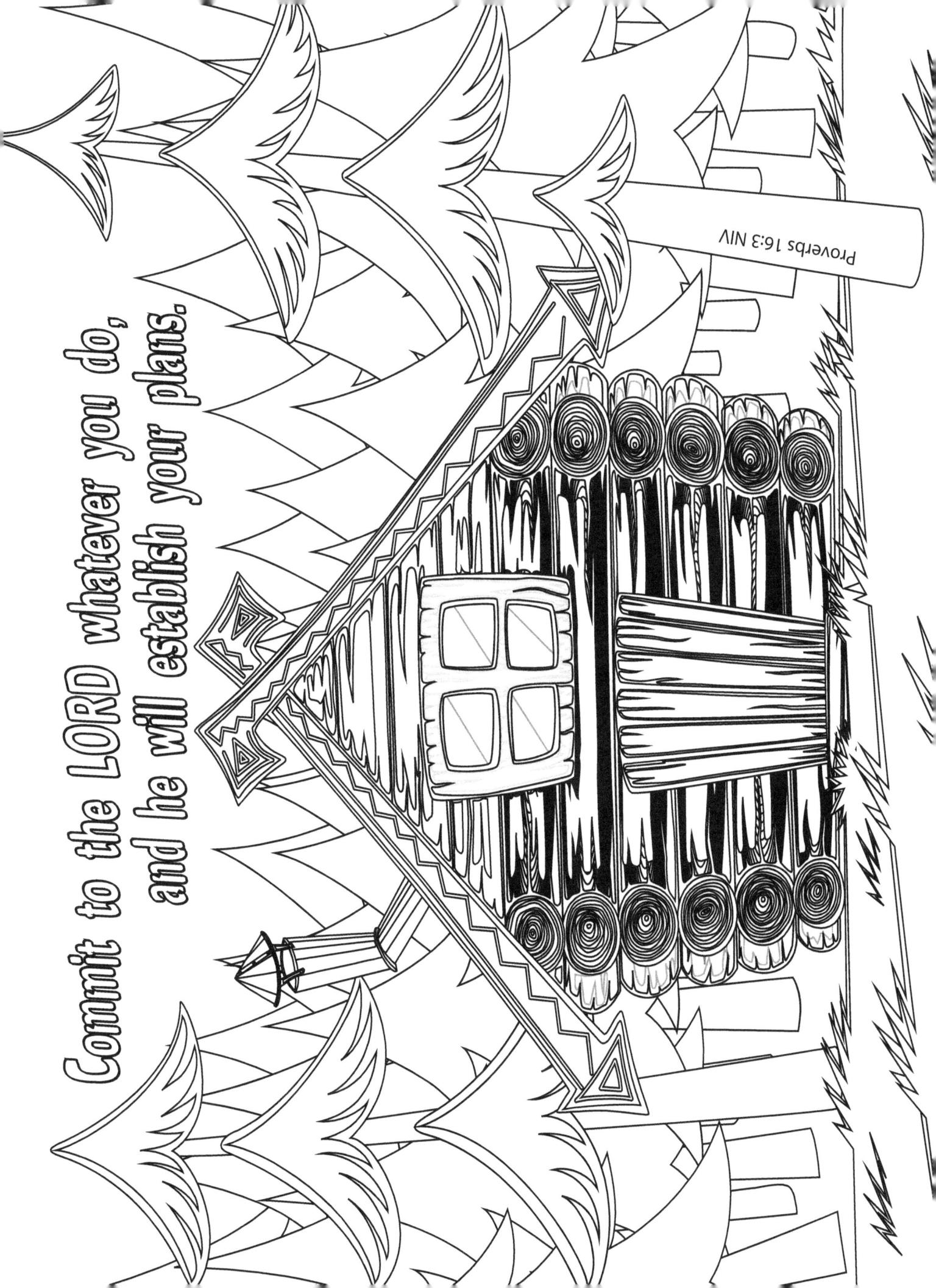

Commit to the LORD whatever you do, and he will establish your plans.

Proverbs 16:3 NIV

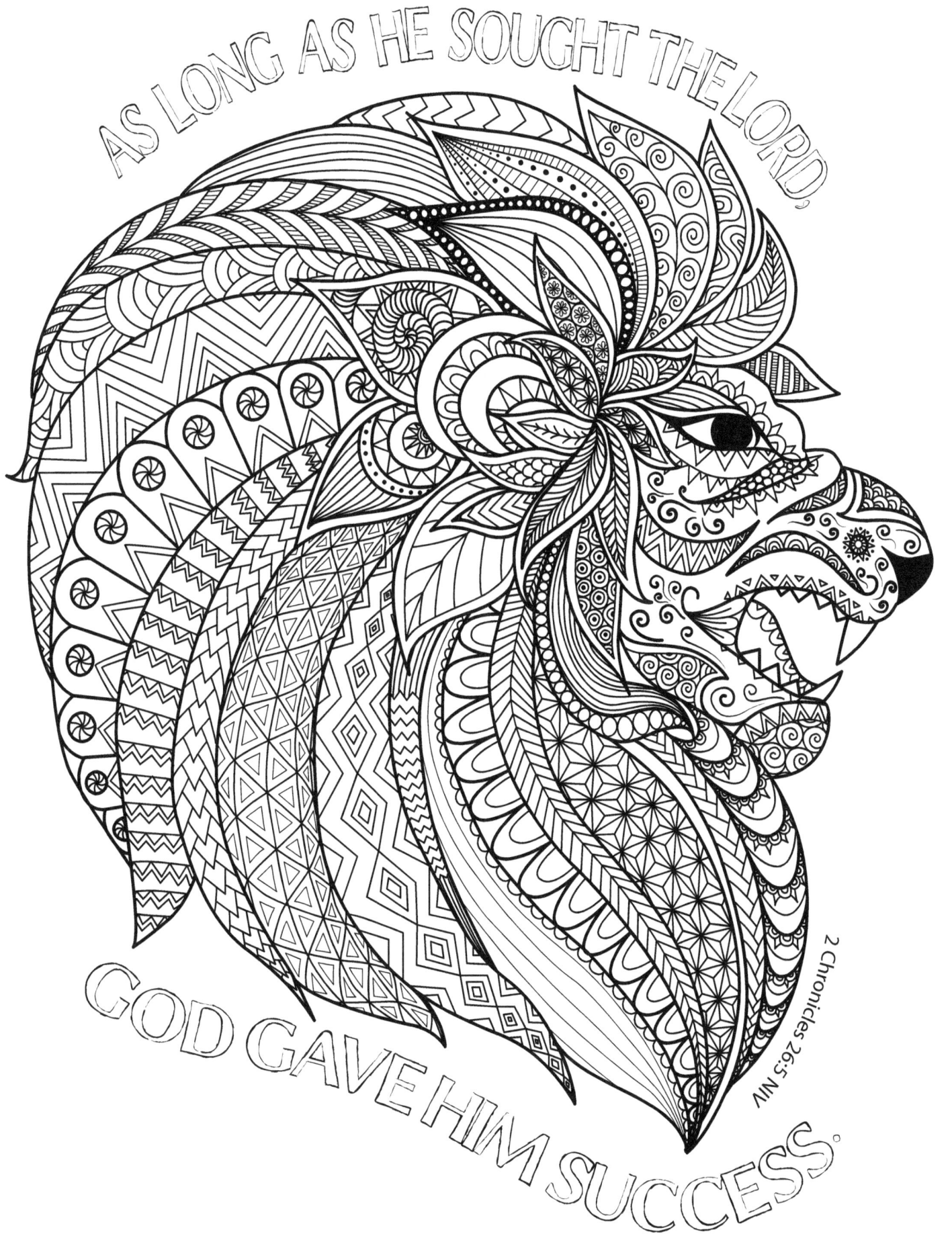

AS LONG AS HE SOUGHT THE LORD,

GOD GAVE HIM SUCCESS.

2 Chronicles 26:5 NIV

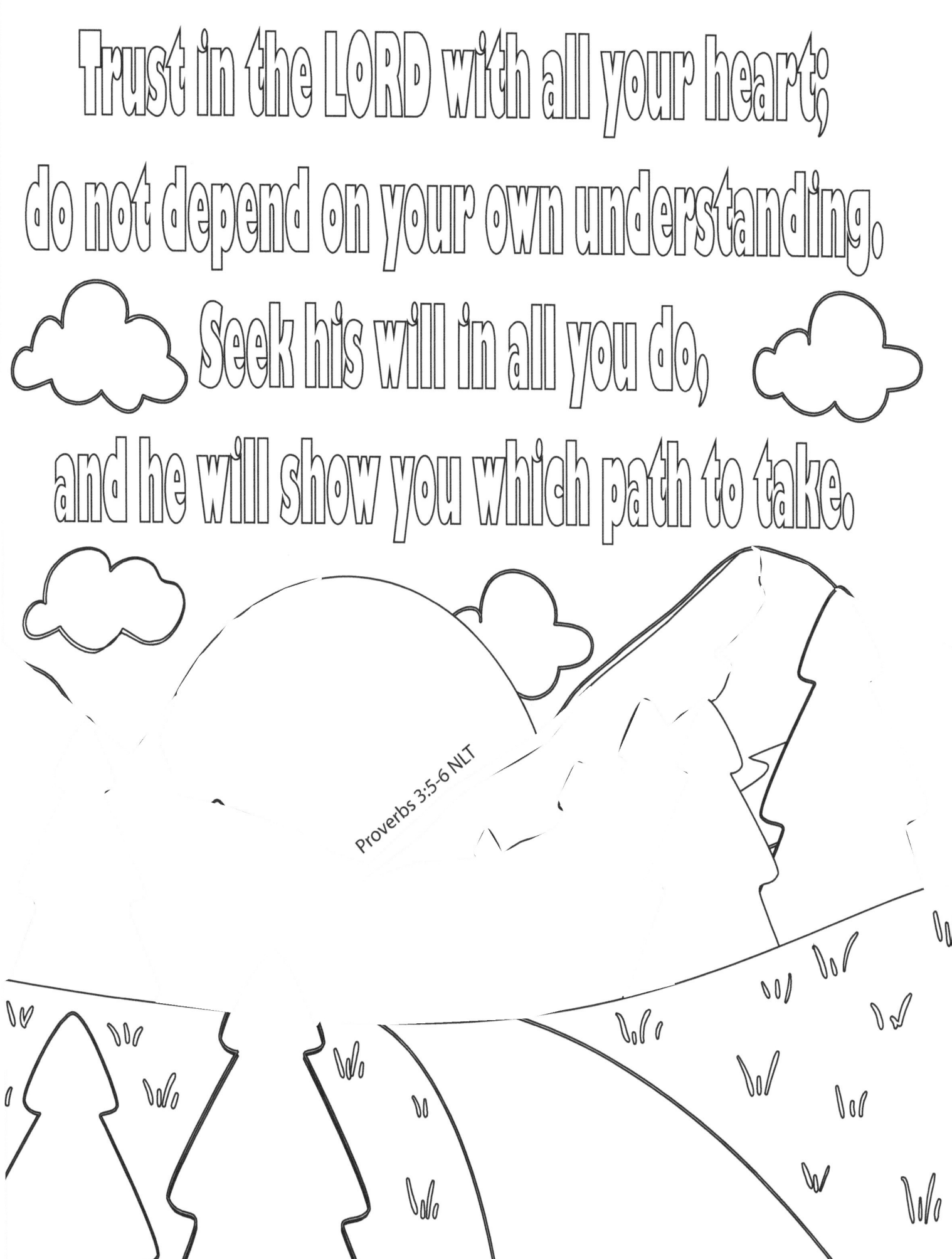

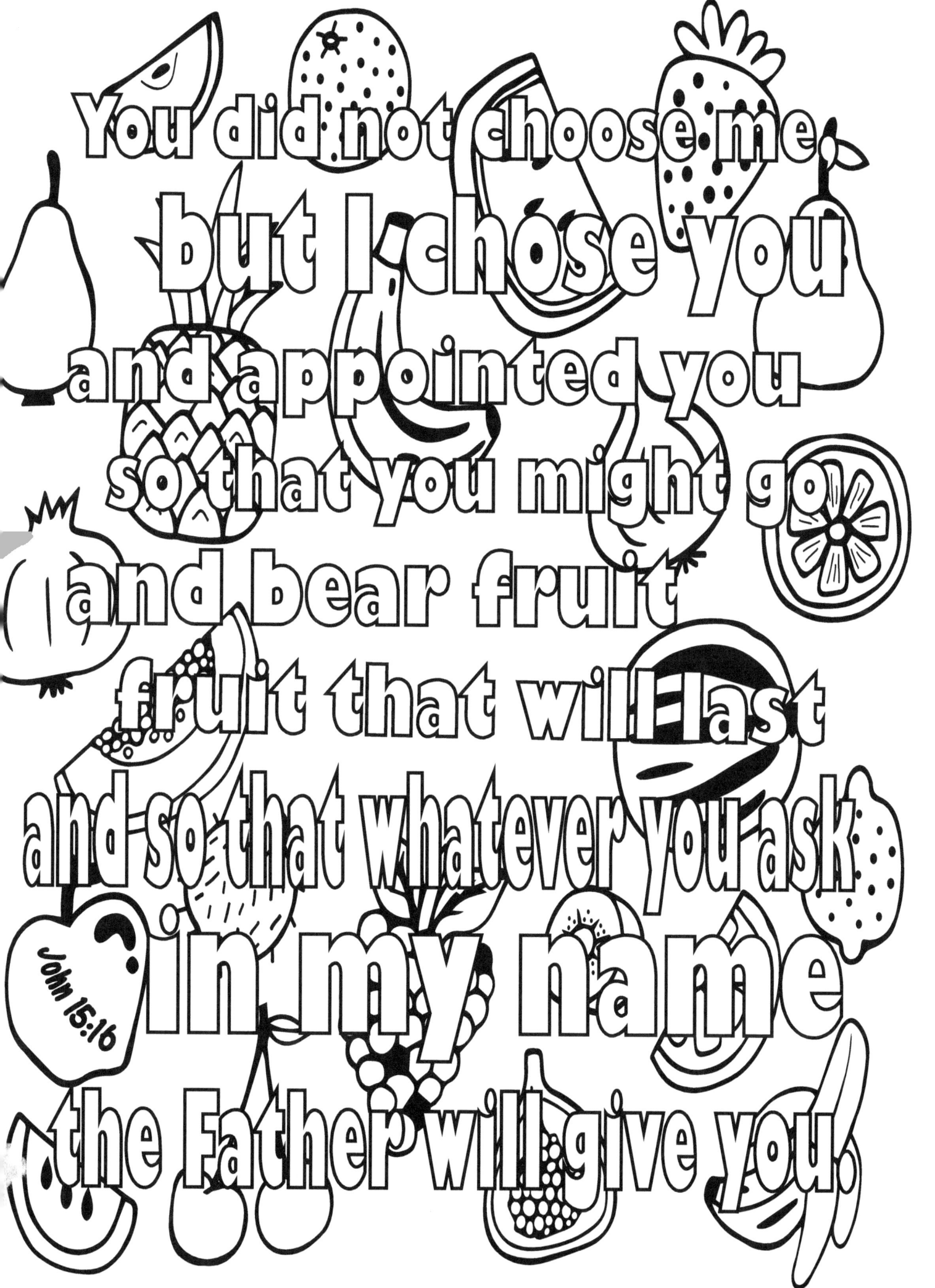

You did not choose me, but I chose you and appointed you so that you might go and bear fruit fruit that will last and so that whatever you ask in my name the Father will give you.

John 15:16

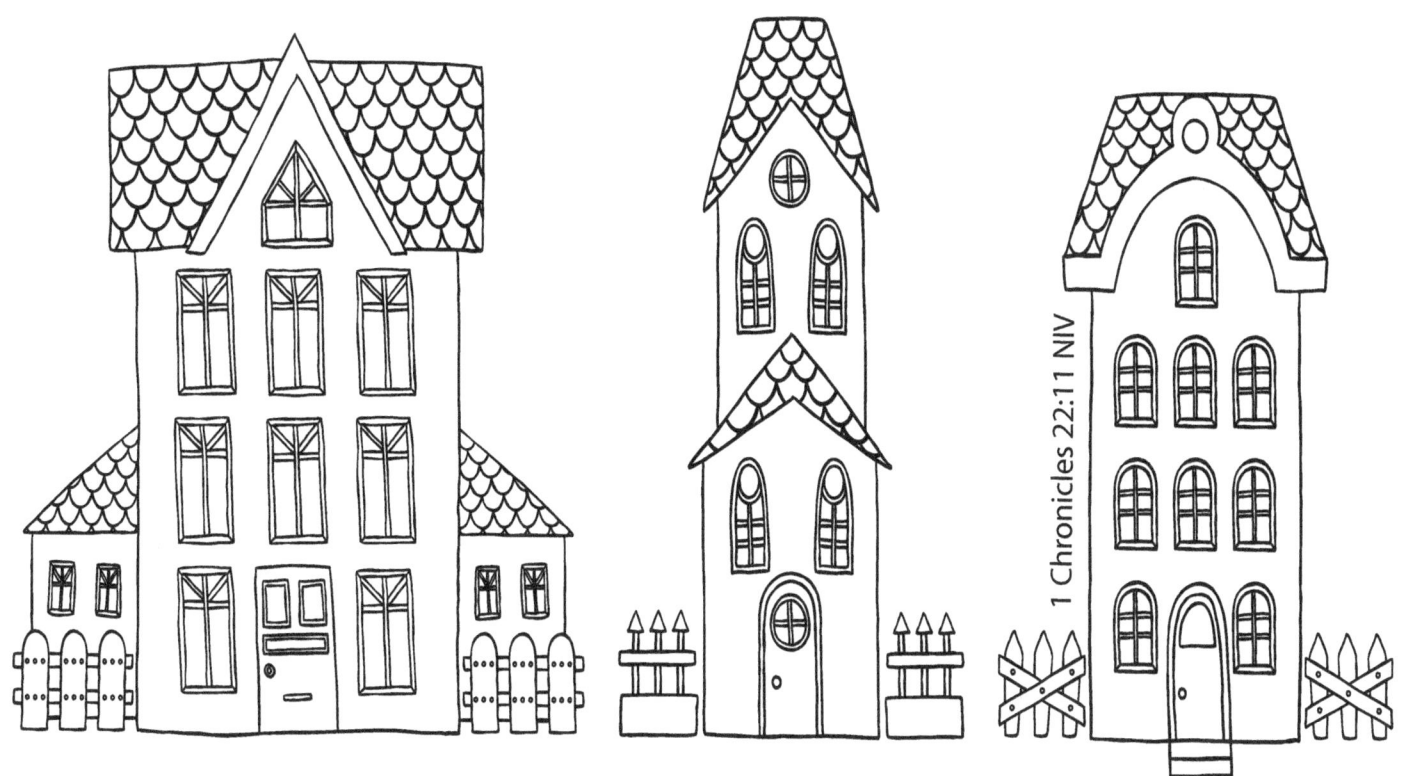

1 Chronicles 22:11 NIV

the LORD be with you,
and may you have success
and build the house of the
LORD your God,
as he said you would.

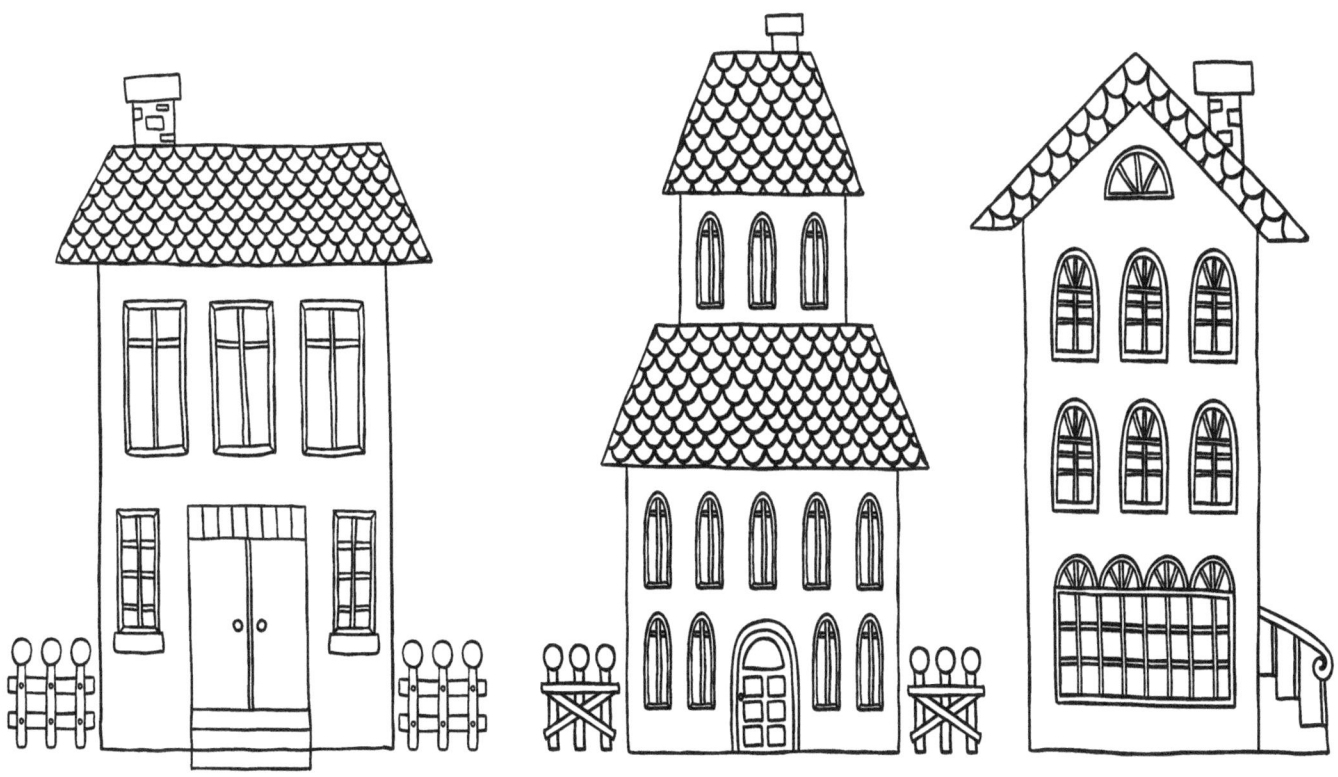

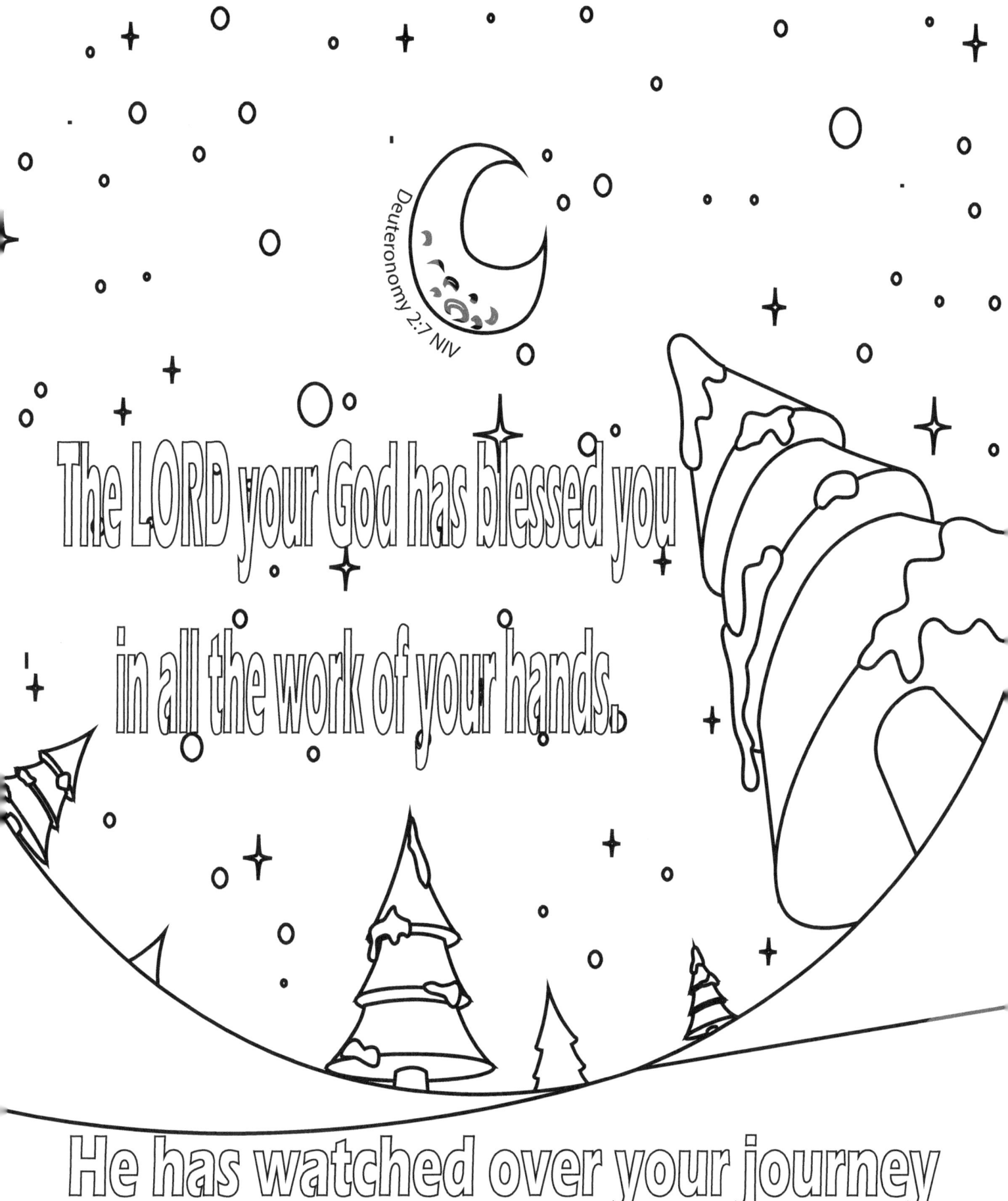

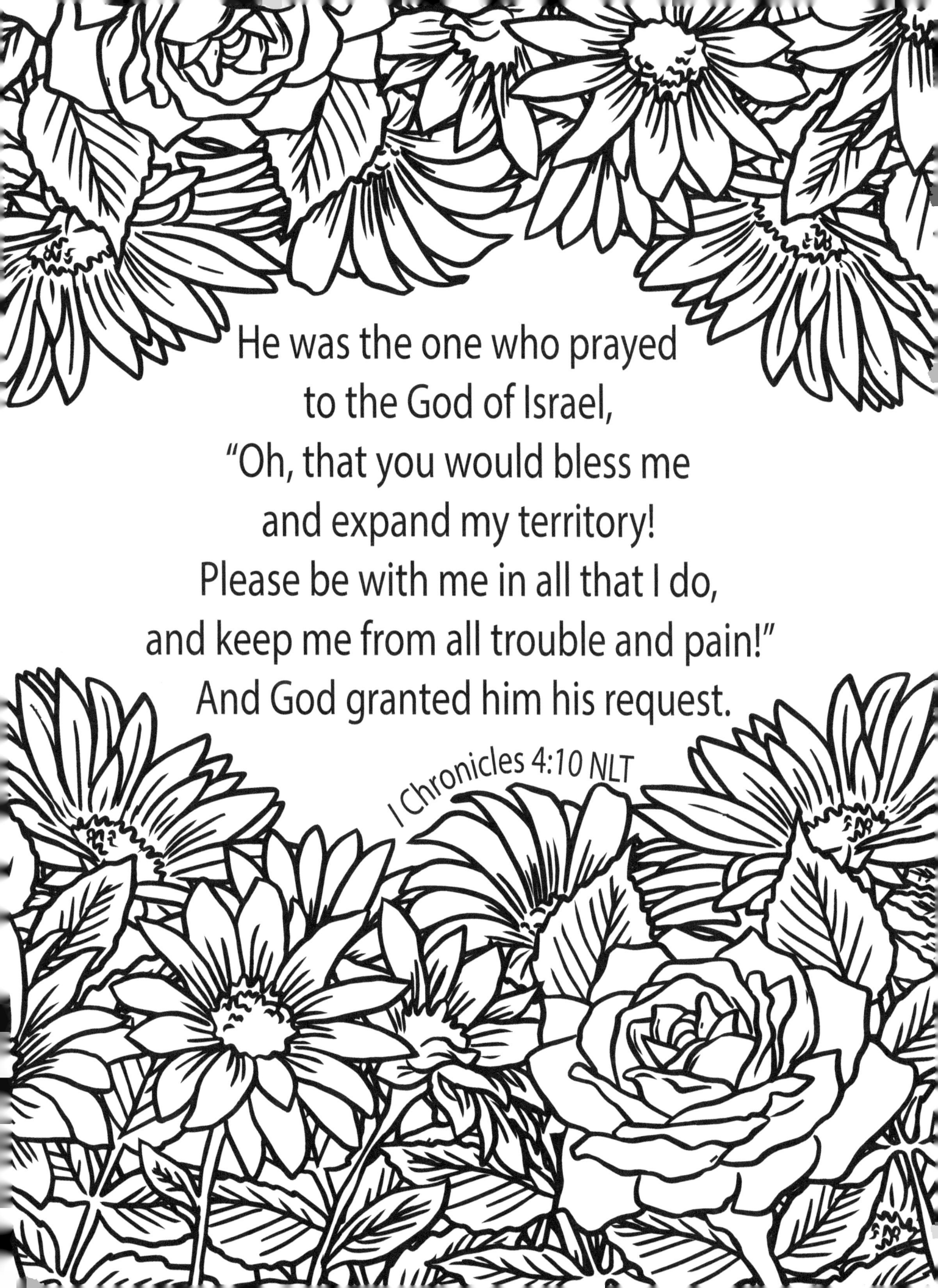

He was the one who prayed
to the God of Israel,
"Oh, that you would bless me
and expand my territory!
Please be with me in all that I do,
and keep me from all trouble and pain!"
And God granted him his request.

I Chronicles 4:10 NLT

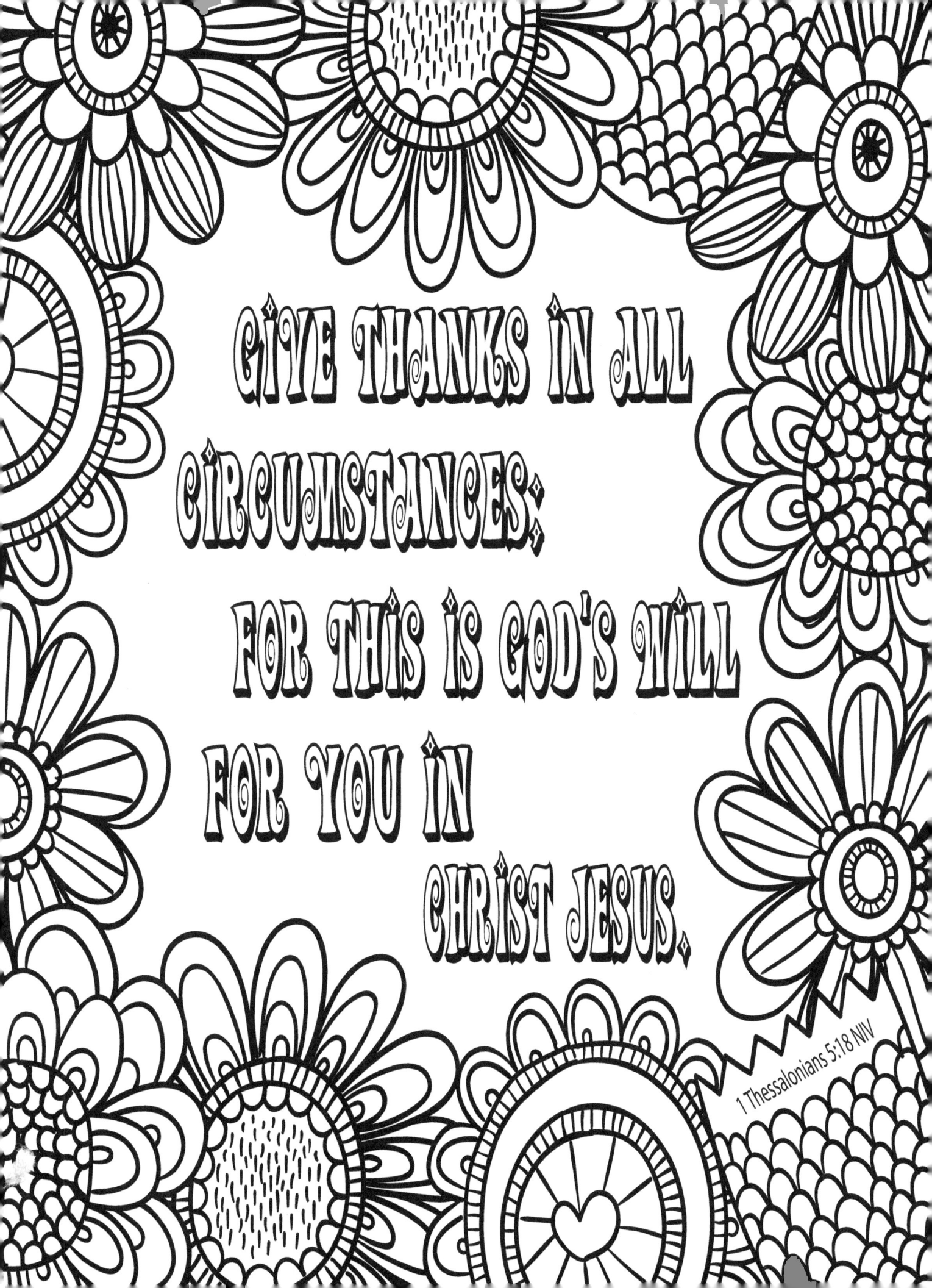

GIVE THANKS IN ALL CIRCUMSTANCES; FOR THIS IS GOD'S WILL FOR YOU IN CHRIST JESUS.

1 Thessalonians 5:18 NIV

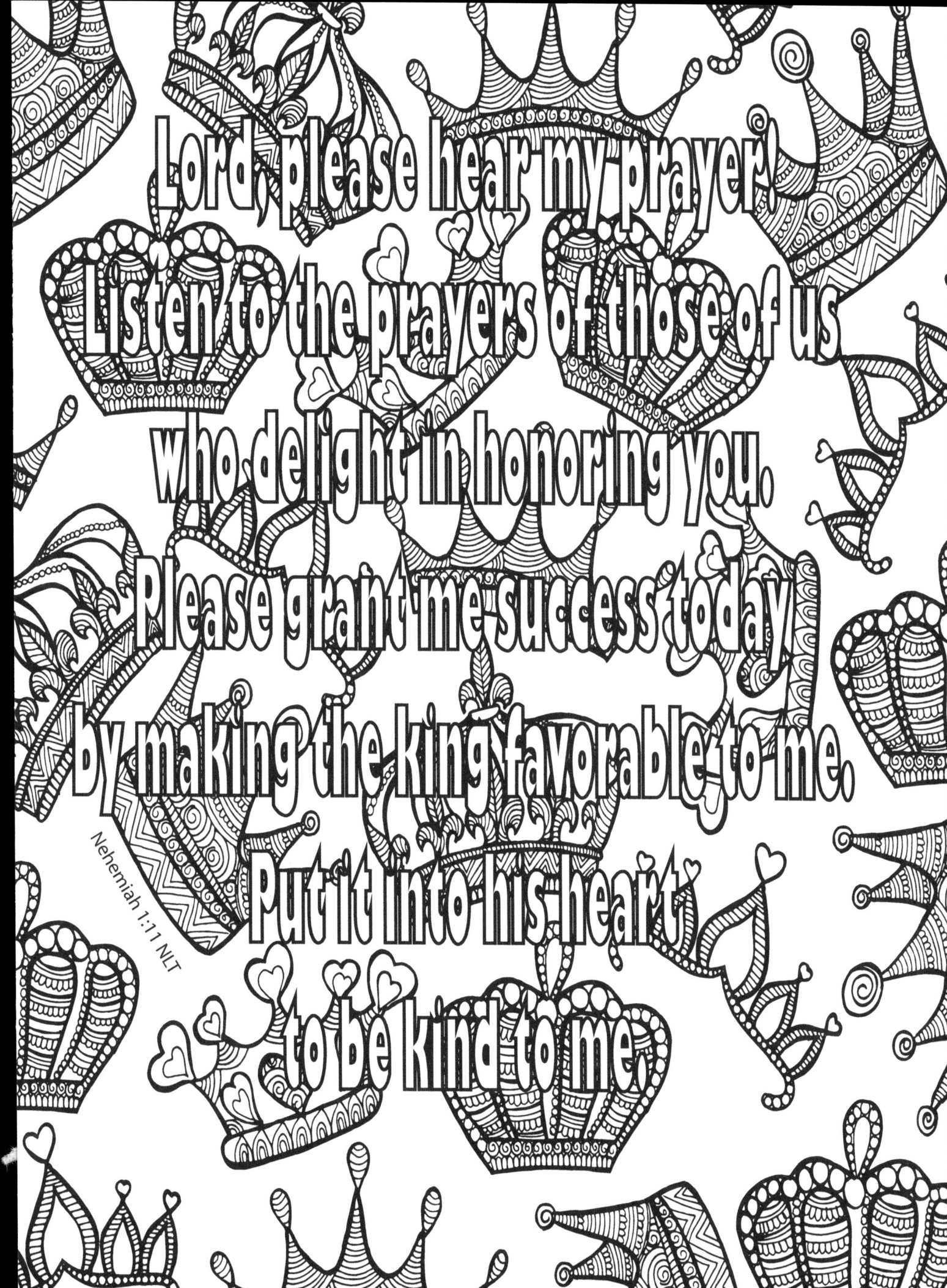

Lord, please hear my prayer!
Listen to the prayers of those of us
who delight in honoring you.

Please grant me success today
by making the king favorable to me.
Put it into his heart
to be kind to me.

Nehemiah 1:11 NLT

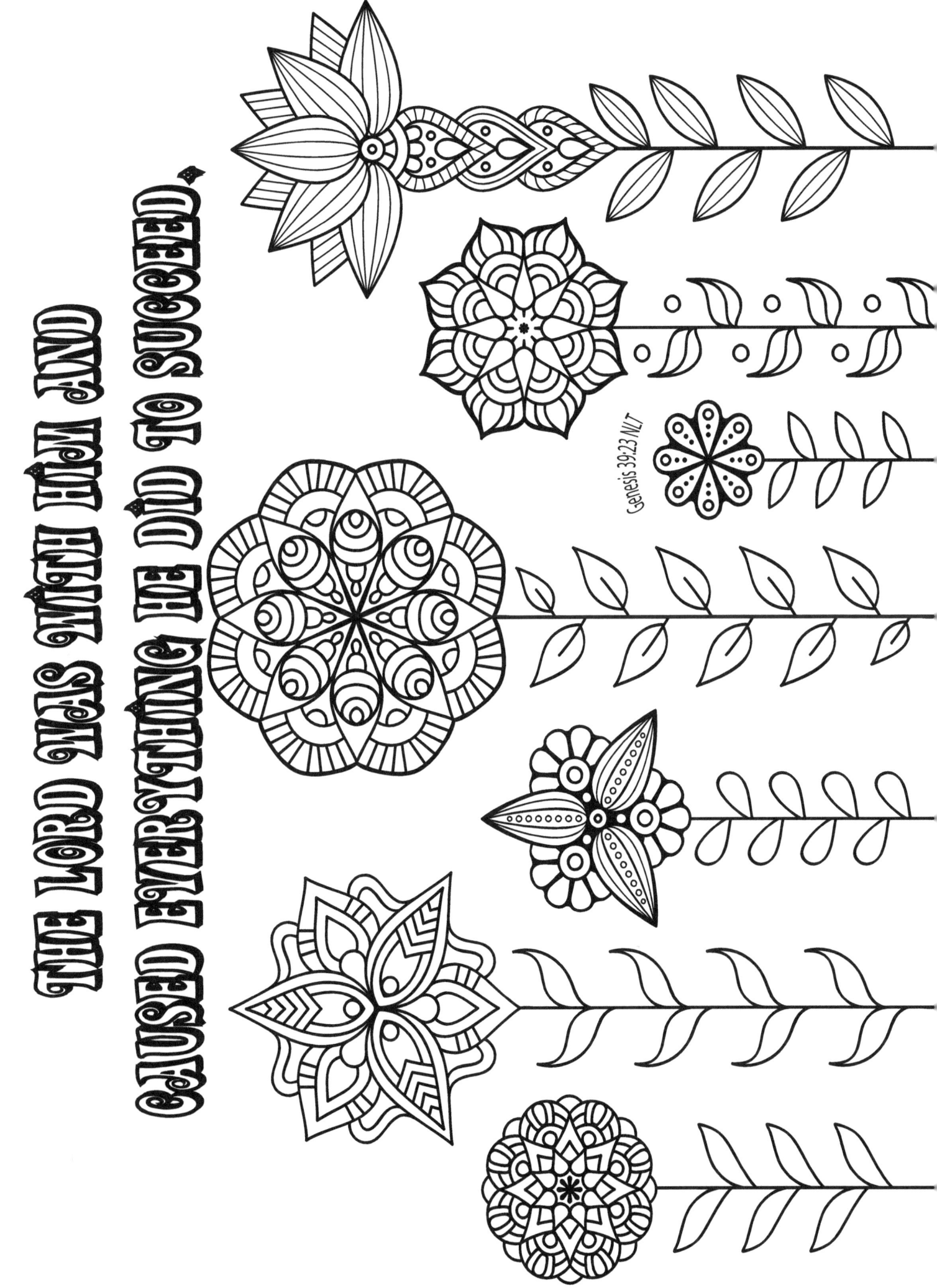

THE LORD WAS WITH HIM AND CAUSED EVERYTHING HE DID TO SUCCEED.

Genesis 39:23 NLT

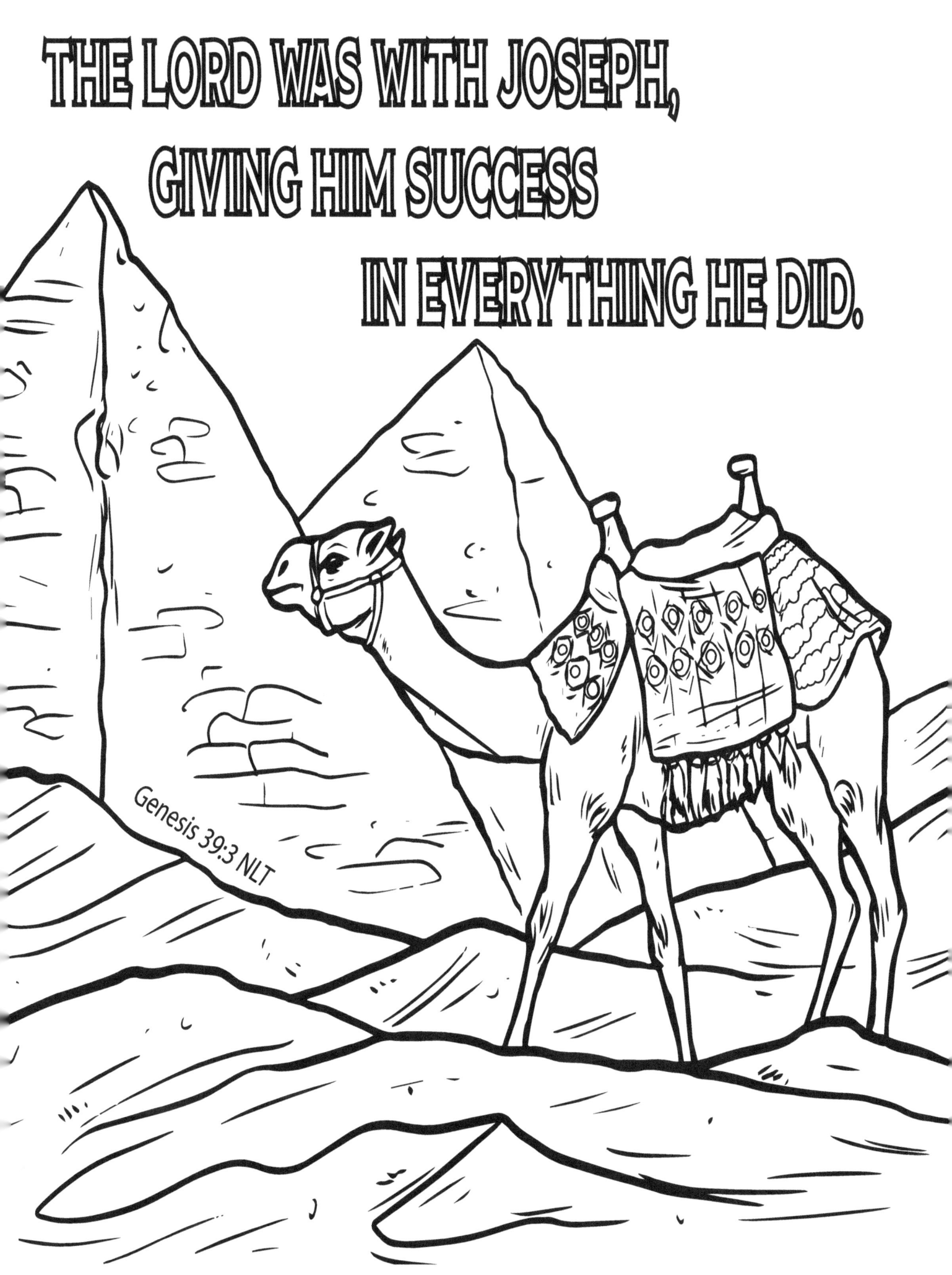

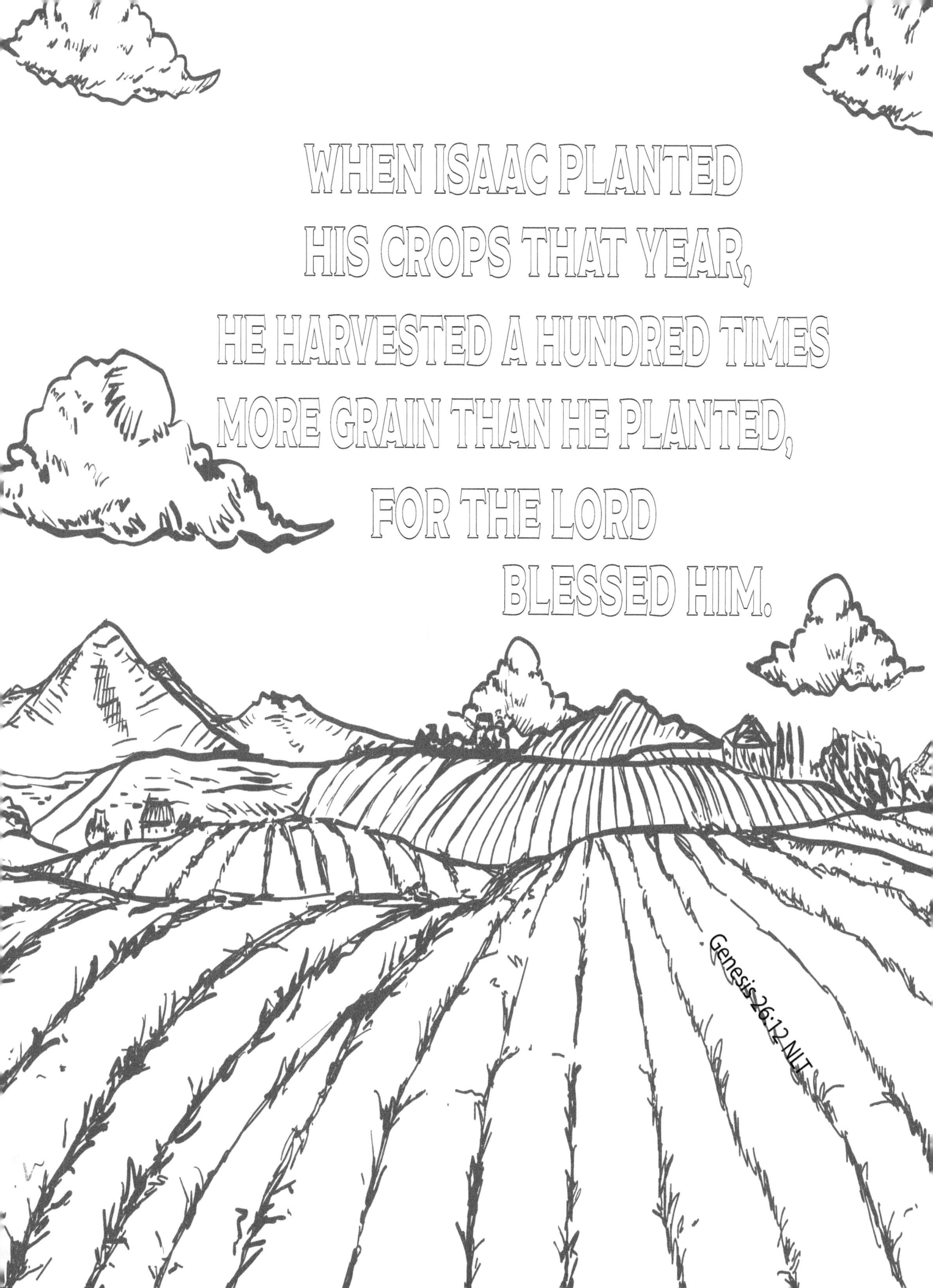

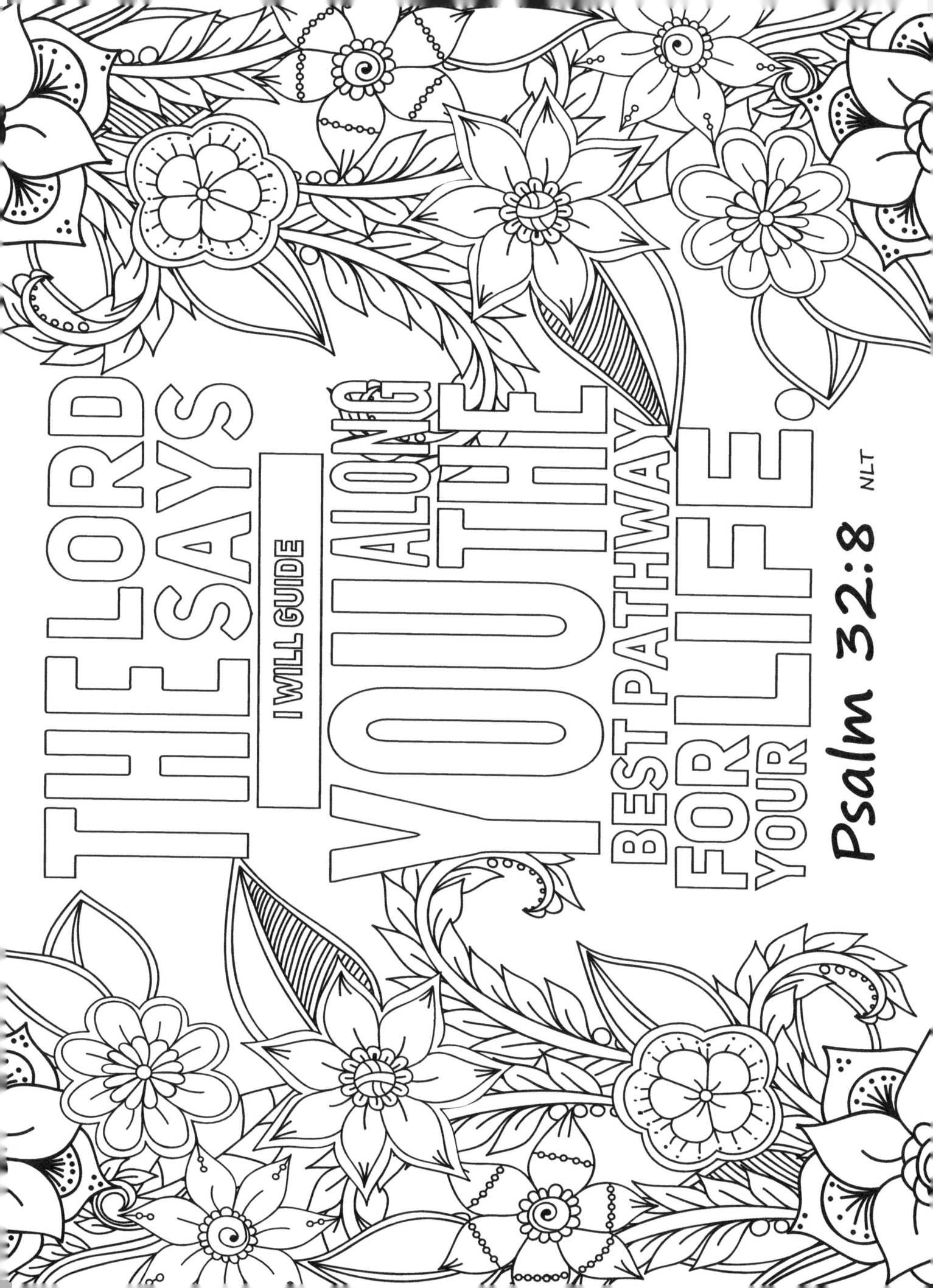

THE LORD THE SAYS I WILL GUIDE YOU ALONG THE BEST PATHWAY FOR YOUR LIFE.

Psalm 32:8 NLT

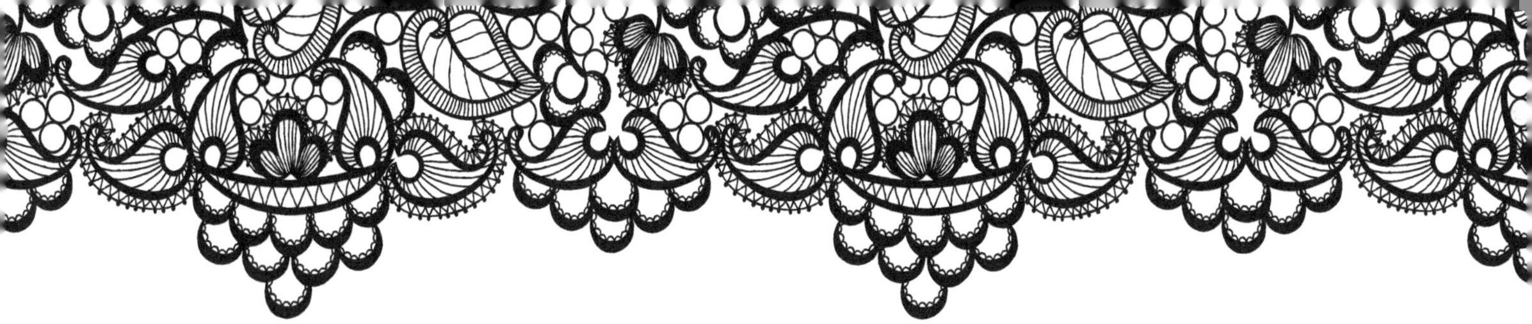

Give generously to them and do so without a grudging heart;
then because of this the LORD your God will bless you in all your work
and in everything you put your hand to.

Deuteronomy 15:10 NIV

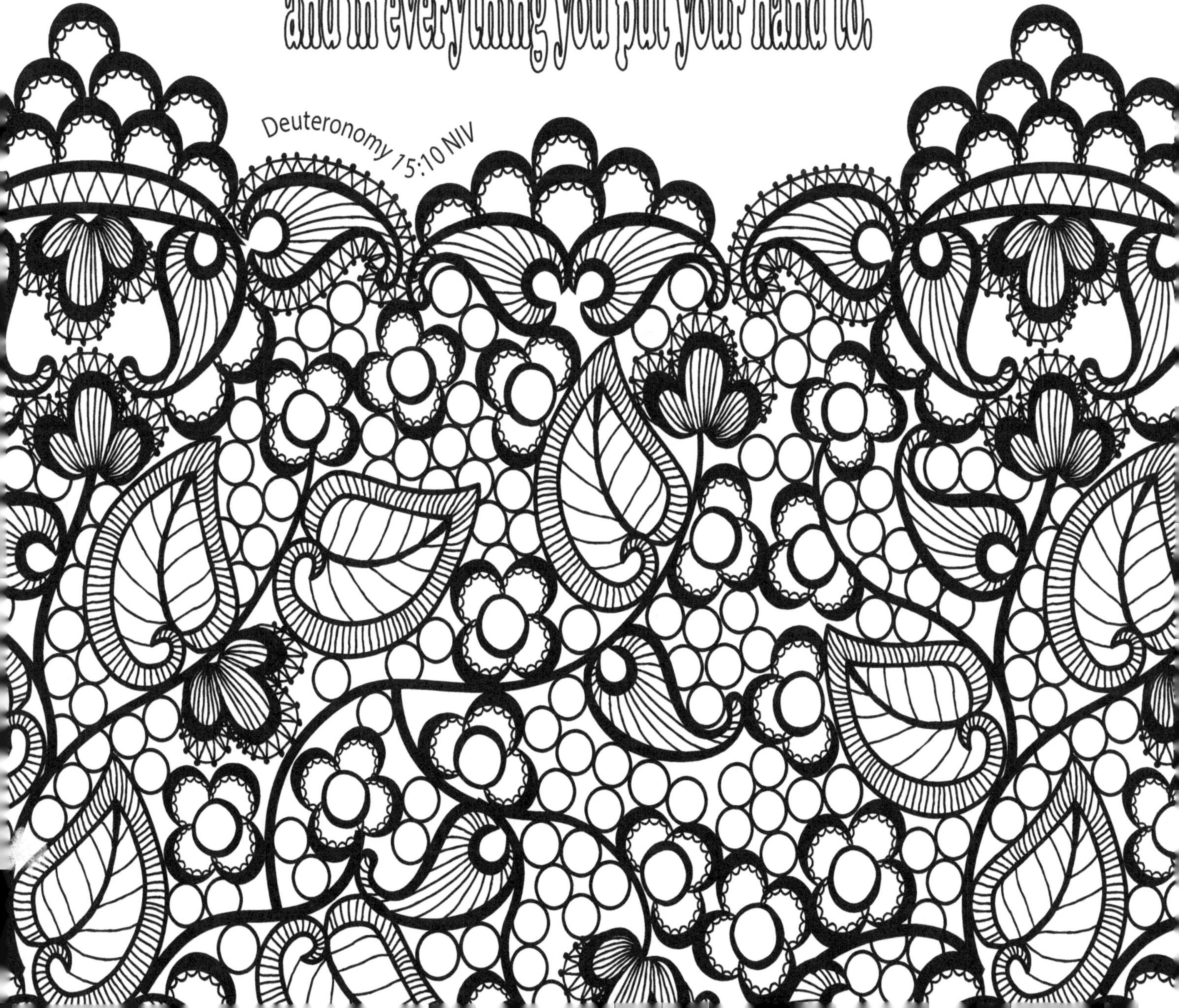

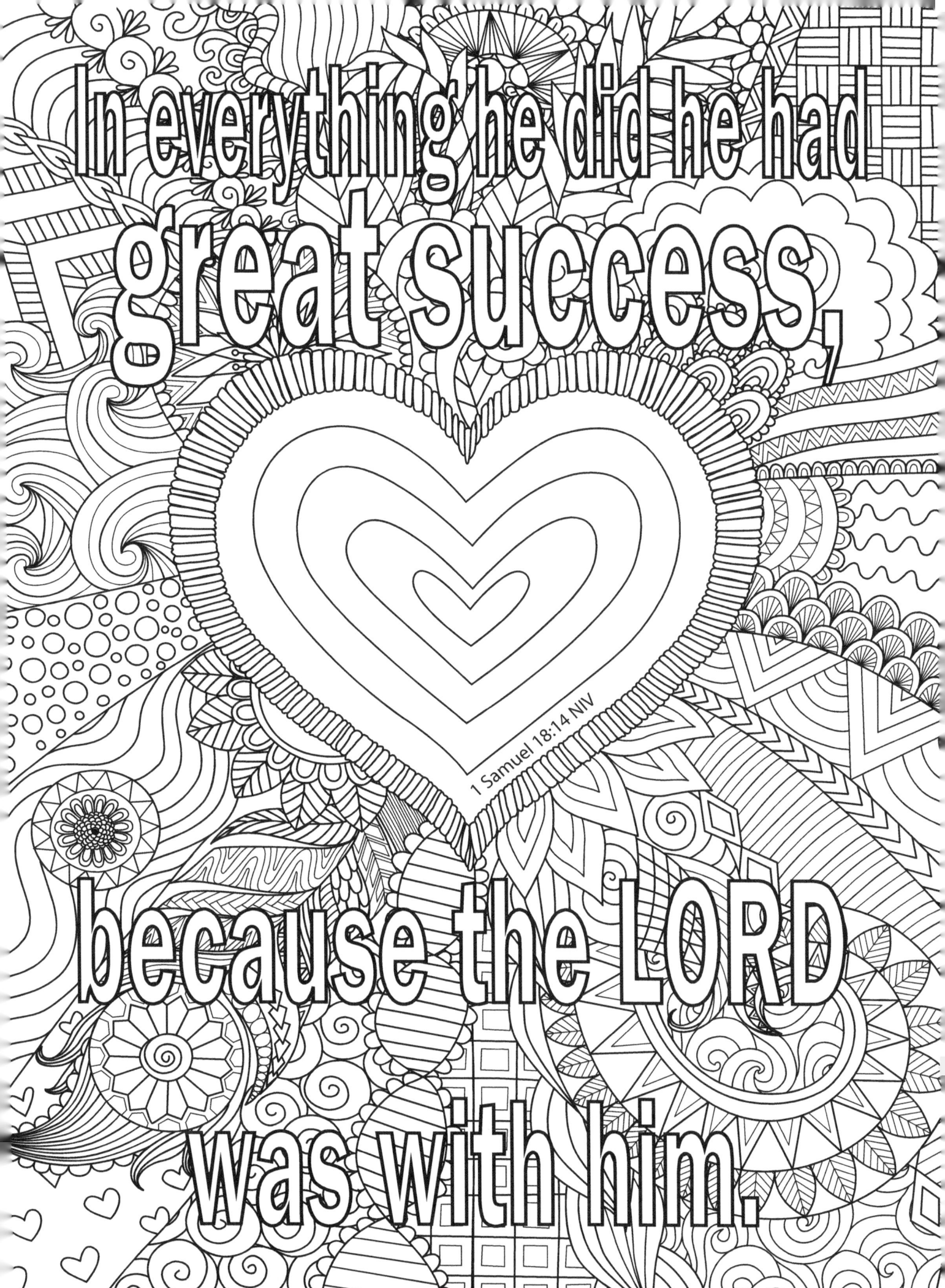

In everything he did he had great success, because the LORD was with him.

1 Samuel 18:14 NIV

The LORD directs the steps of the godly. He delights in every detail of their lives.

Psalm 37:23 NLT

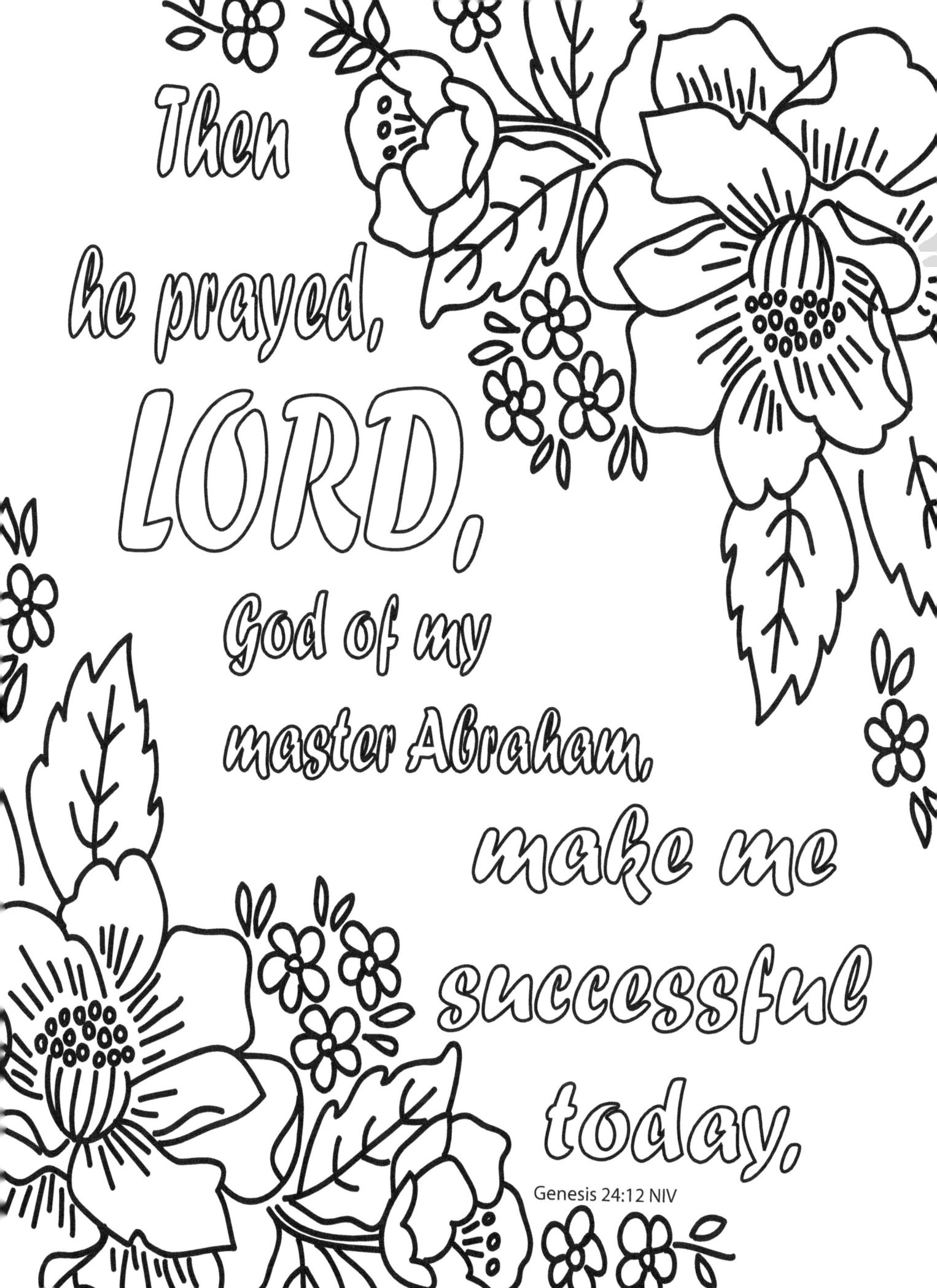

Then he prayed, LORD, God of my master Abraham, make me successful today.

Genesis 24:12 NIV

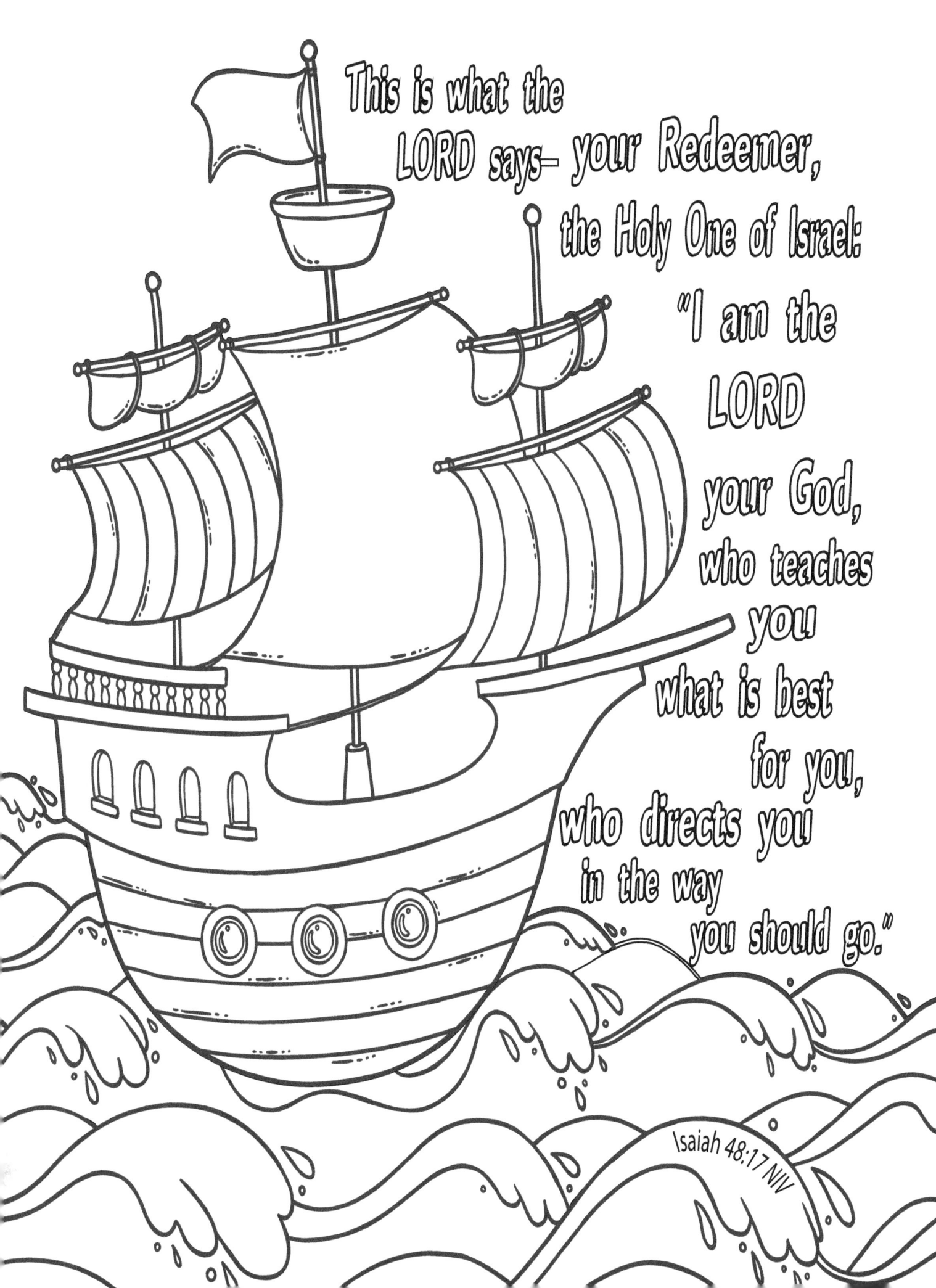

This is what the LORD says— your Redeemer, the Holy One of Israel: "I am the LORD your God, who teaches you what is best for you, who directs you in the way you should go."

Isaiah 48:17 NIV

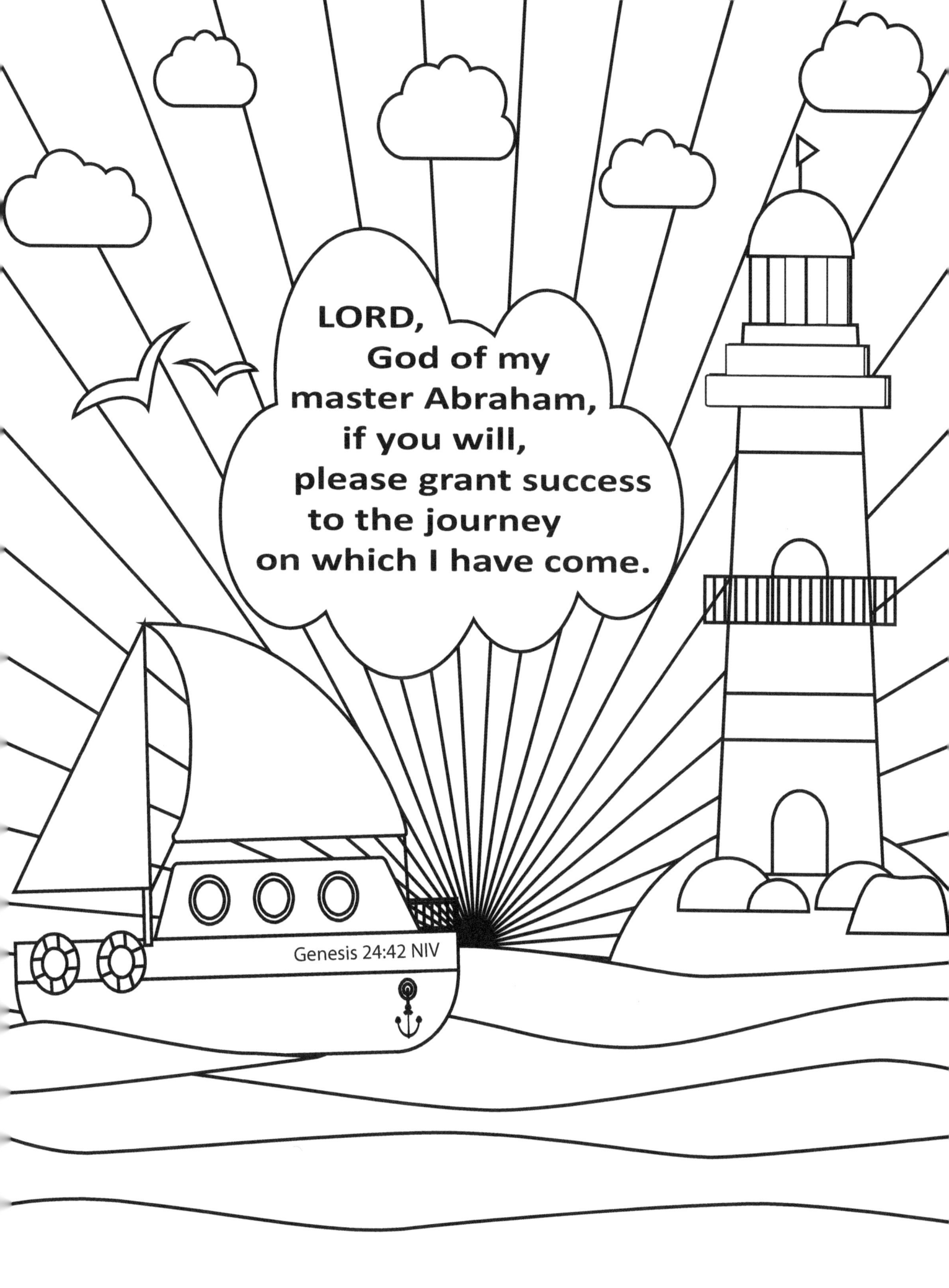

LORD,
God of my
master Abraham,
if you will,
please grant success
to the journey
on which I have come.

Genesis 24:42 NIV

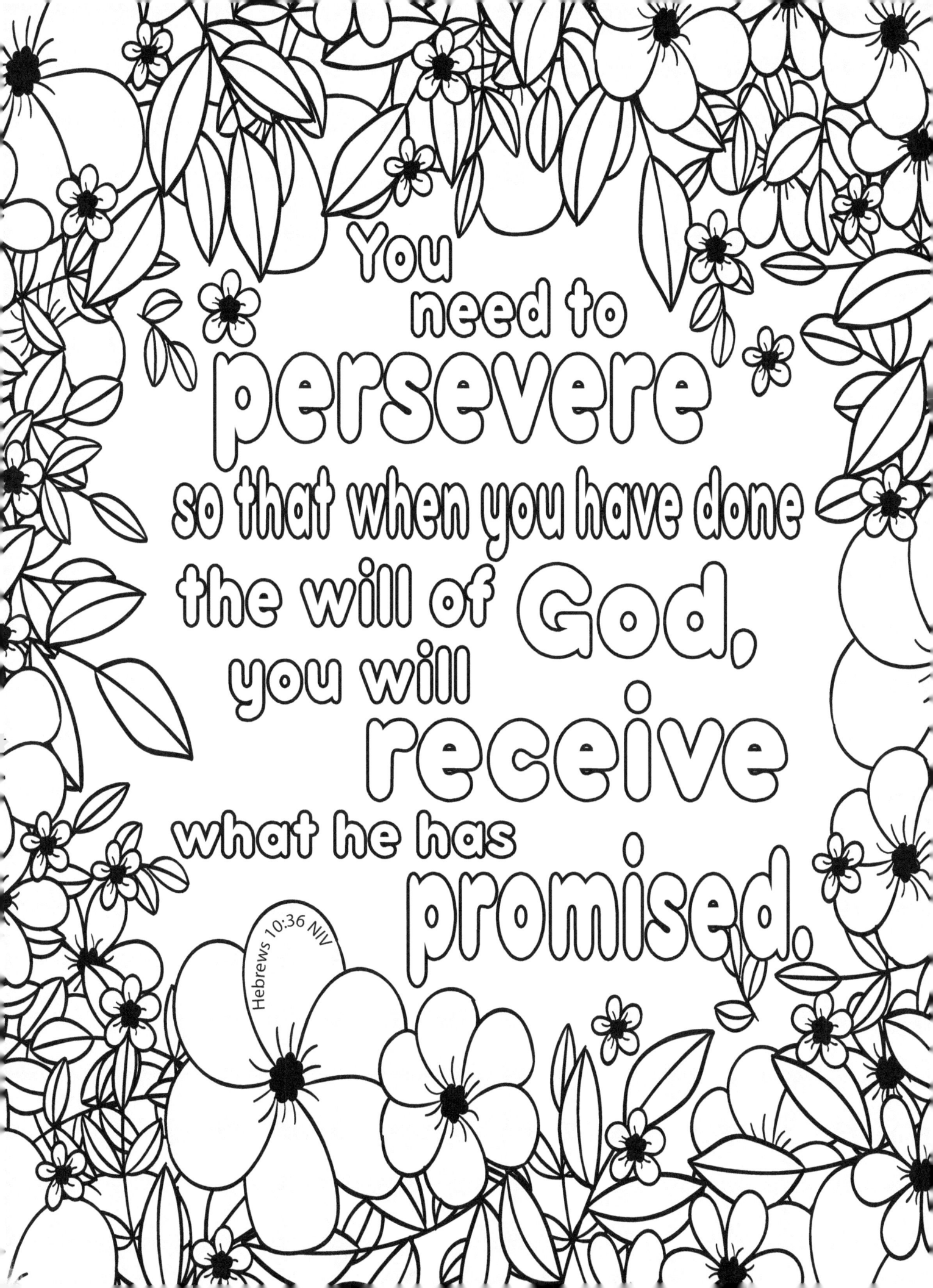

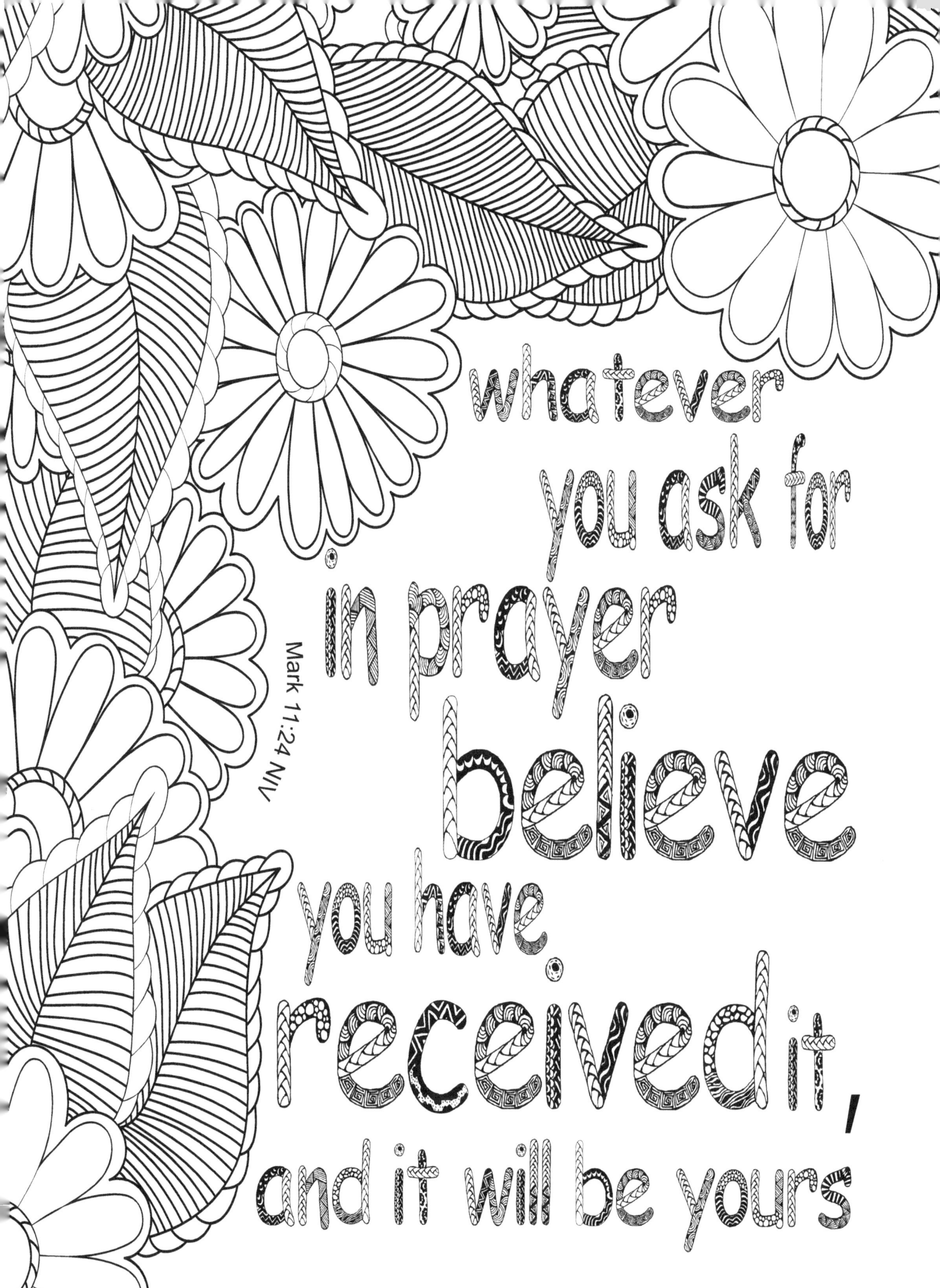

whatever you ask for in prayer believe you have received it, and it will be yours

Mark 11:24 NIV

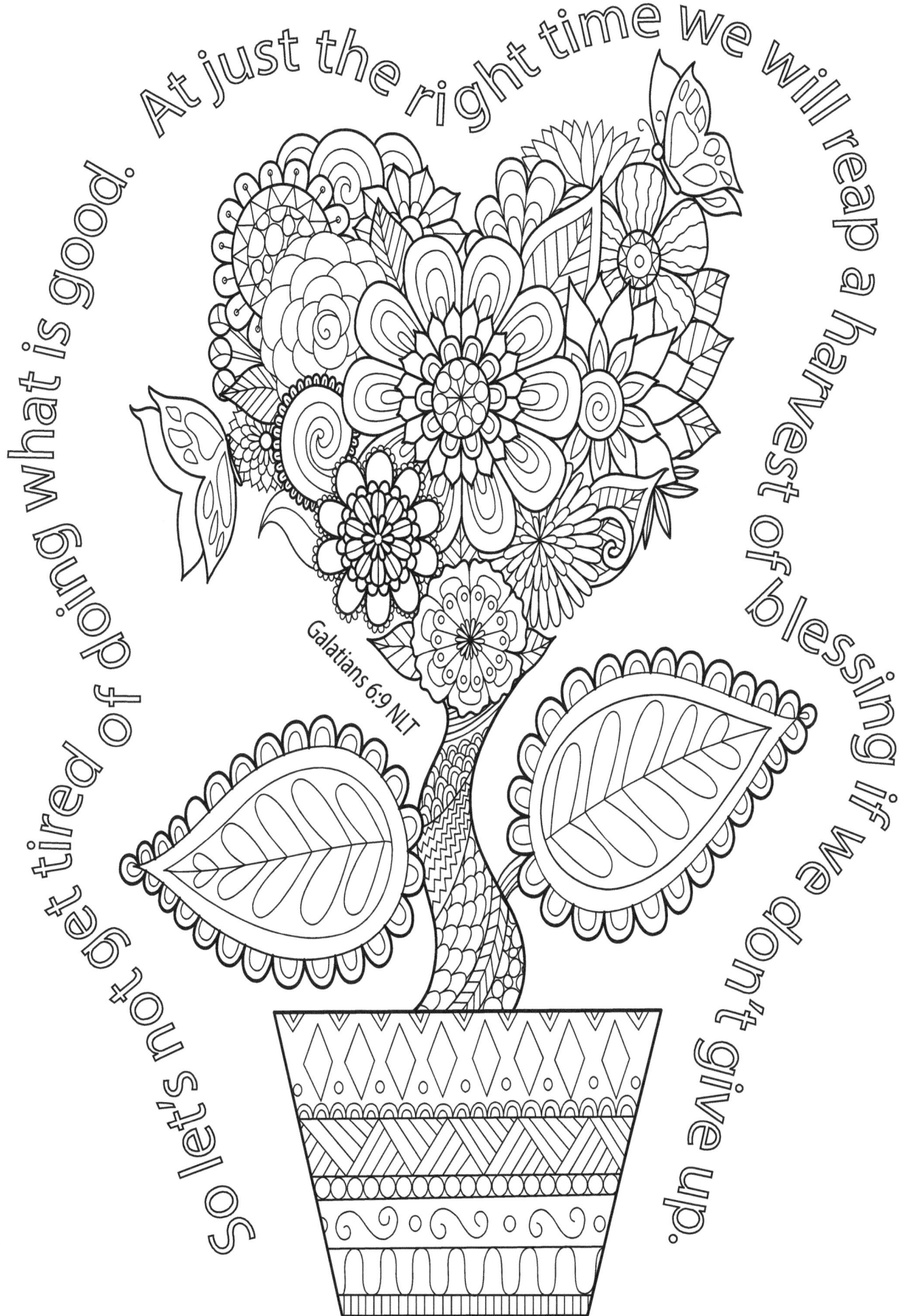

So let's not get tired of doing what is good. At just the right time we will reap a harvest of blessing if we don't give up.

Galatians 6:9 NLT

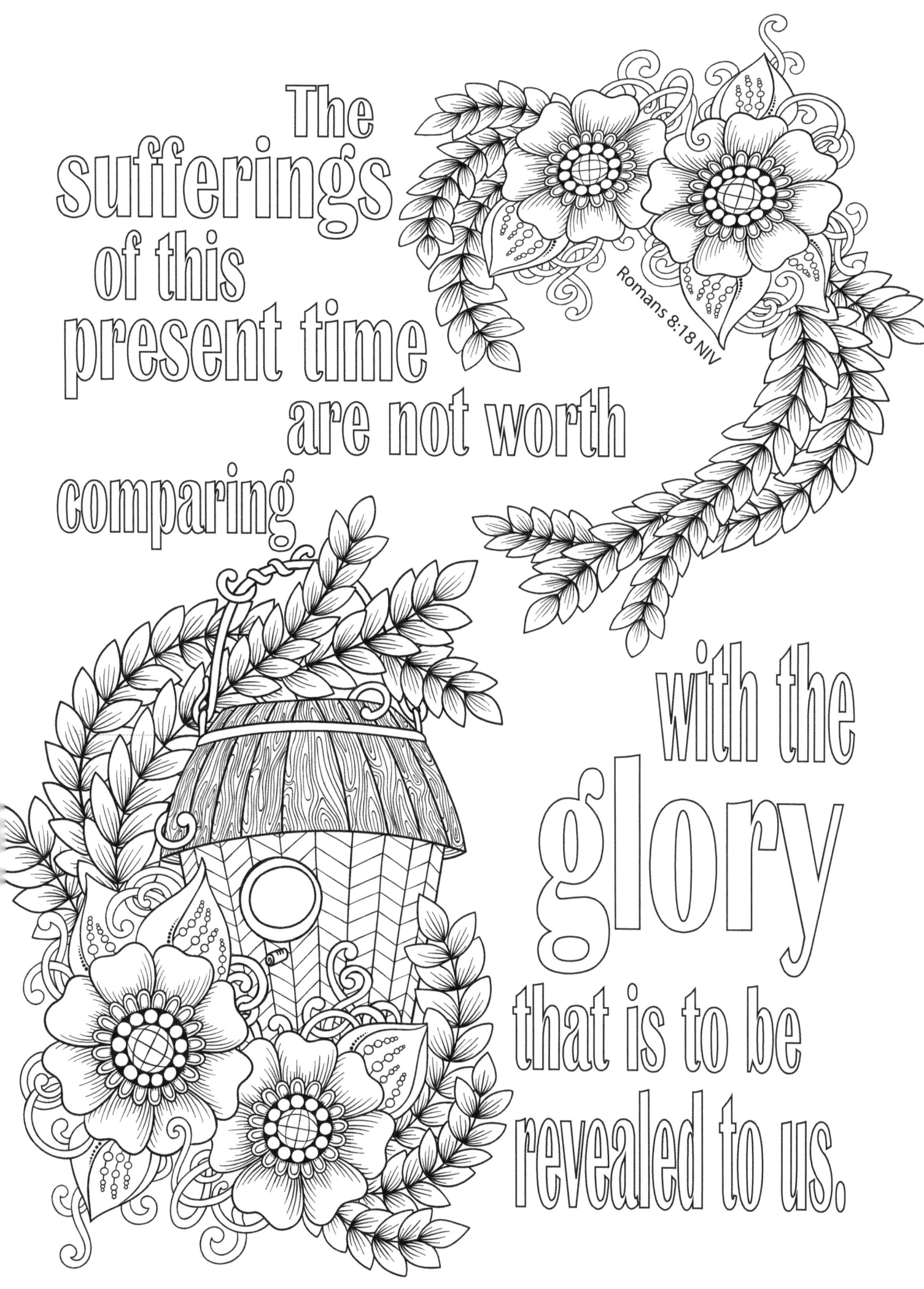

The sufferings of this present time are not worth comparing

Romans 8:18 NIV

with the glory that is to be revealed to us.

BLOTTING PAGE

Use This Page To Prevent Marker Bleed Through. Or To Test
And Keep Track Of Your Color Selections So You Can Pick
Just The Right Colors Or Not Forget Which Ones You Were Using.

BLOTTING PAGE

Use This Page To Prevent Marker Bleed Through. Or To Test
And Keep Track Of Your Color Selections So You Can Pick
Just The Right Colors Or Not Forget Which Ones You Were Using.

BLOTTING PAGE

Use This Page To Prevent Marker Bleed Through. Or To Test
And Keep Track Of Your Color Selections So You Can Pick
Just The Right Colors Or Not Forget Which Ones You Were Using.

BLOTTING PAGE

Use This Page To Prevent Marker Bleed Through. Or To Test
And Keep Track Of Your Color Selections So You Can Pick
Just The Right Colors Or Not Forget Which Ones You Were Using.

BLOTTING PAGE

Use This Page To Prevent Marker Bleed Through. Or To Test
And Keep Track Of Your Color Selections So You Can Pick
Just The Right Colors Or Not Forget Which Ones You Were Using.

BLOTTING PAGE

Use This Page To Prevent Marker Bleed Through. Or To Test
And Keep Track Of Your Color Selections So You Can Pick
Just The Right Colors Or Not Forget Which Ones You Were Using.

BLOTTING PAGE

Use This Page To Prevent Marker Bleed Through. Or To Test
And Keep Track Of Your Color Selections So You Can Pick
Just The Right Colors Or Not Forget Which Ones You Were Using.

BLOTTING PAGE

Use This Page To Prevent Marker Bleed Through. Or To Test
And Keep Track Of Your Color Selections So You Can Pick
Just The Right Colors Or Not Forget Which Ones You Were Using.

BLOTTING PAGE

Use This Page To Prevent Marker Bleed Through. Or To Test
And Keep Track Of Your Color Selections So You Can Pick
Just The Right Colors Or Not Forget Which Ones You Were Using.

BLOTTING PAGE

Use This Page To Prevent Marker Bleed Through. Or To Test
And Keep Track Of Your Color Selections So You Can Pick
Just The Right Colors Or Not Forget Which Ones You Were Using.

BLOTTING PAGE

Use This Page To Prevent Marker Bleed Through. Or To Test
And Keep Track Of Your Color Selections So You Can Pick
Just The Right Colors Or Not Forget Which Ones You Were Using.

BLOTTING PAGE

Use This Page To Prevent Marker Bleed Through. Or To Test
And Keep Track Of Your Color Selections So You Can Pick
Just The Right Colors Or Not Forget Which Ones You Were Using.

BLOTTING PAGE

Use This Page To Prevent Marker Bleed Through. Or To Test
And Keep Track Of Your Color Selections So You Can Pick
Just The Right Colors Or Not Forget Which Ones You Were Using.

BLOTTING PAGE

Use This Page To Prevent Marker Bleed Through. Or To Test
And Keep Track Of Your Color Selections So You Can Pick
Just The Right Colors Or Not Forget Which Ones You Were Using.

BLOTTING PAGE

Use This Page To Prevent Marker Bleed Through. Or To Test And Keep Track Of Your Color Selections So You Can Pick Just The Right Colors Or Not Forget Which Ones You Were Using.

BLOTTING PAGE

Use This Page To Prevent Marker Bleed Through. Or To Test And Keep Track Of Your Color Selections So You Can Pick Just The Right Colors Or Not Forget Which Ones You Were Using.

BLOTTING PAGE

Use This Page To Prevent Marker Bleed Through. Or To Test
And Keep Track Of Your Color Selections So You Can Pick
Just The Right Colors Or Not Forget Which Ones You Were Using.

BLOTTING PAGE

Use This Page To Prevent Marker Bleed Through. Or To Test
And Keep Track Of Your Color Selections So You Can Pick
Just The Right Colors Or Not Forget Which Ones You Were Using.

BLOTTING PAGE

Use This Page To Prevent Marker Bleed Through. Or To Test
And Keep Track Of Your Color Selections So You Can Pick
Just The Right Colors Or Not Forget Which Ones You Were Using.